Hand Of Hope
The Story Behind The Picture

Michael Clancy

To Erica

Blessings

Michael Clancy

DEDICATION

This book is dedicated to my father, Ed Clancy. I love you more
than you could ever know.

CONTENTS

FORWARD

Wow...what an honor! If I'd been told 18 years ago I would be writing a forward for Michael Clancy, I wouldn't have believed it. But, here I sit, typing away, still in shock, and thrilled at the opportunity!

Michael was "THE" Photography Department at the Review Appeal Newspaper in Franklin, TN. I began working in the Circulation Department in 1993. Our paths crossed seldom, but enough to notice each other's work ethics. He always arrived early, left late, and worked hard. He was dedicated, determined, and professional; a true "perfectionist" from the word go. (I believe in today's terminology they call it obsessive/compulsive). He was passionate about his work. He's a hard person to get to know, but understandable once you know his story. Of course, his shyness doesn't help matters much either.

As life would have it, our paths parted, and years passed. I moved around and wound up in Florida. However, I stayed in contact with my old boss from the Review, Don Anderson, throughout the years. We hadn't spoken for a few months, when he called. He asked if I remembered a Michael Clancy that used to be the photographer at the newspaper.

"Sure, I do", I responded. And he told me how they had re-connected.

A few months later, Don came down to visit. He had a golf buddy in the area and they planned to play golf and to go to the Concours D'Elegance Car Show. Once he arrived he gave me a copy of a photo Michael had taken...when I opened the package I cried. The photo was of a small child's hand holding the gloved finger of his doctor while still in the womb. I had seen a similar photo, which I later learned was quite often mistaken as Michael's. I kept this photo above my bed and couldn't help but cry every time I stopped to look at it. I don't remember sharing this with anyone at the time, but I was hurting and angry. My daughter had recently suffered a miscarriage. I felt so helpless. We went from the excitement of preparing for a new addition, to the loss of a loved one we would never hold. The photo reminded me of just how fragile and precious life is.

Time passed, and it was Thanksgiving weekend. Don called and said, "Guess where I am?" He loved playing games. "I give up. Where are you?" I said. He responded, "I'm at Michael's visiting the horses. Here...you two should talk." Yep.... just like that..... no warning, just put us on the phone together. Needless to say, it was a brief first conversation.

Soon Michael and I began corresponding via email, and eventually chatting on the phone. I wanted to know more about this incredible photo. How did he manage to get such an unbelievable shot? Why would the doctor deny the obvious? Who could keep quiet about such an amazing event? Why didn't any of the nurses speak up? How could anyone see this photo and still choose to end the life of an innocent child? Yes...Michael was hit with a barrage of questions. I read his website, but I still wasn't satisfied. The more he shared the more I wanted to know.

The story is so multi-faceted. It covers deception, denial, abuse, hatred, forgiveness, loneliness, life, death, truth, love, perseverance, and much more. I suggest keeping tissues near by as you read. You will see how God had His hand all over Michael preparing him for the walk of faith he has lived for the past 12 years.

As time rolled along, and many conversations later, Michael informed me he had started writing a book. He had completed 8 chapters. I told him I couldn't wait to read it! But to my surprise, he was so discouraged thinking it wasn't worth finishing. No one seemed to want to know the truth about what happened in that operating room. For a man, who never had any children of his own, to witness such a wonderful and miraculous site was completely overwhelming. But, it seemed the more he tried to tell his story, the more people wanted to keep him quiet. He almost convinced himself nobody cared about what really happened. I told him, I DID!

It's taken over three years of coaxing, but he finally broke and decided the story needed to be shared. YEHAW! In his heart, he knew it had to be told. He didn't have a support system, someone to encourage him. That is, until I came along and flooded him with motivation. (Actually, I believe the word he used to describe it was "nagging"!!) What he considered "nagging" I considered loving, gentle nudges, clothed with stern encouragement.

Maybe I should explain how I gained those nagging rights...uh...I mean nudging rights. Well, you see, our relationship developed to the point we were talking everyday, and reading the Bible together each night. We started discussing how to reach more people, researching and interviewing folks for the book, and how to better organize event scheduling. We held a lot of "business" meetings over the phone and through emails. Finally, I told Michael I would be willing to help him any way I could. But he said it would be next to impossible with me living so far away. I volunteered to move back to Tennessee. He thought I was joking. (Bet he won't make that mistake again!)

After a few weeks, I made a trip to Tennessee to begin the search for a job. I located a position with a company in the same field I was currently in – Property Management. I loved my job in Florida. I was the CAM Administrative Coordinator for Amelia Island Management. To land a job so similar was an absolute blessing and miracle! Michael was in shock I found a job, and so quickly. (Truth be told, he was shocked I was actually moving to Tennessee to help him). After locating a job, I lined up a place to live, contacted the PODS Company, and had the packing day all planned. But as with all well made plans, Satan threw in some monkey wrenches just for kicks. Too many to list right now, but believe me, he gave me a run for my money.

I headed to Mobile, AL for a short visit with my mom, and contacted my new boss to inform her I would be in town within a few days.

I made it to Tennessee the same day Michael was returning from an event in Grand Rapids, MI. It was Wednesday, September 24, 2008. I'll never forget that day. I was full of mixed emotions. I left my mom with a bad feeling her health was much worse than she led me to believe. I was looking forward to my new job. I was missing my grandson, daughter, son, and friends I left behind in Florida. And, I was extremely nervous yet, excited about working with Michael. But, the real reason I'll never forget that date is because that very day Michael asked me to marry him! We married one week later on October 2, 2008, granting me my nudging rights. Well deserved, I think.

The first few months of our marriage were very busy and full of trying times. Michael had a full schedule of events. As a matter of fact, we married on Thursday, and he flew out Friday morning for an event in Beckley, WV. I found out the owner of Preferred Property Management gave my job to one of her friends who was recently laid off. I was devastated, and worried. My mom's health worsened. I spent a lot of time traveling back and forth to Mobile. Within two and a half months, on December 28, 2008, I lost my mother to cancer. Michael was an absolute Godsend through it all.

We started discussing our plans for the book, events, and he shared more of the story. He pulled up hundreds of emails he'd received, and began reading them to me. I was completely heartbroken by one he read where a nurse carried babies in her scrubs pocket just to allow them some human contact before they passed away! I cried for days after that one. I kept visualizing a tiny, innocent child struggling to survive.

Michael pulled out boxes upon boxes of items relating to the photo. I was amazed at the amount of documentation he'd kept over the years. Much of it you will learn about as you read his account of things. This book cannot contain everything because there's just too much to cover.

I watch Michael struggle daily to keep up with answering emails. If one comes in the middle of the night he gets up to read it. He doesn't want anyone to have to wait for a response. It hasn't been easy, but God has truly blessed us. Granting us strength, perseverance, and understanding. He knew when, where, and how this story would come together.

I believe, as you read this book you will come to know, and understand Michael in a much better light than ever before. He may not be a polished speaker, or an accomplished writer, but his story is real, honest, and compassionate. This book is written in his own words, by his own hands. I hope it will become evident the battle he chose to fight was not one for himself but for others. The guilt he bears over not being able to spare his siblings the pain and abuse they suffered compelled him to never let the innocent go without a voice again.

Michael and I know God brought us together to spread His word concerning the innocent, the unborn, the silenced. He has walked with us through some very dark, hard, scary times but He always made our path clear. As you read this book you will feel His presence. This is God's story. To God be the Glory, Amen! - Juanita Clancy

1 BEHIND CLOSED DOORS

It was the first day of July 1999. A select few at Vanderbilt University Medical Center were reeling from the news they were going to be featured on the cover of the Millennium Issue of Life Magazine. Dr. Joseph Bruner was the most excited of all. He pioneered a new medical procedure to correct spina bifida on a baby, still in it's mother's womb. This procedure was the focus of the upcoming Life Magazine article titled, "Born Twice."

The editors planned an incredible picture for the cover. Today, July 1, 1999, Max Aguilera-Hellweg entered Dr. Bruner's operating room with a stepladder, and a 4 x 5 camera on a tripod. He was able to get an unbelievable shot of the outstretched arm of twenty-four week in utero, Sarah Marie

Switzer, for the cover. This could possibly be the most controversial issue Life Magazine has ever published.

Everyone at Vanderbilt saw the picture Max took and were elated. It was the perfect cover.

Imagine the excitement you would have if you were going to be part of this story. The cover of Life Magazine, this would be Dr. Bruner's crowning glory. The publicity would also be great for the hospital, the fetal surgery program, and even great for the city of Nashville.

I ruined all that. This is my story, in my own words.

I was a geeky kid. I wore a lot of sweaters. I even wore those fake turtlenecks, and penny-loafer shoes. I had an old cruiser bicycle with a basket on the handlebars I rode everywhere. It came in handy for my newspaper route.

I had two great friends when we lived in Rock Island, Illinois, Dave Stone, and Brian Coberly. We met at Washington Junior High School and became inseparable.

A popular thing was collecting beer cans. You could not have two alike. The most I ever had, one hundred, twenty-two. That was a small collection compared to some of the guys I knew. Our old house was so rickety if you shut a door a little too hard downstairs, my beer-can collection would come tumbling down with a thunder. I stacked them pyramid style.

We lived at 2552 20th Avenue North. My older sister, Trish, had her bedroom in the basement, along with a den, and laundry room. My younger sister, Michelle, had a bedroom on the second floor. My brother, David, and I shared a bedroom, also on the second floor. Our parents' room was in the middle. Late one night I saw my stepfather tiptoe past our door as he went downstairs. He was naked. I didn't want to see him and quickly turned away. He and my mom were avid readers and drank beer as they read every night. He always drank too much.

Our stepfather was the local Navy Recruiter.

One day, I got home from school before my siblings. I entered the back porch and a gallon of white paint had fallen off a shelf. The lid came off, spilling paint everywhere. David and Michelle got home shortly after. My stepfather had been home for some time and today he was very drunk. Us kids knew to stay out of sight when he was like this.

I was trying to clean up the paint and he saw me. He freaked! "Who did this!" he yelled. I told him it happened before we came home. He acted as if he didn't believe me. He got his belt and lined us up. He grabbed my little sister, Michelle, and started hitting her with the belt across her legs saying, "I'm going to whip all of you until I find out who spilled the paint."

I remember the red marks he was leaving and how I wanted to stop him. More than anything in the world, I wanted to stop him.

"I did it!" I yelled, "It was an accident!" He glared at me as if I was ruining his fun. He stopped and let go of her. He stumbled to the stairs.

I went outside to get away. Our German shepherd was in the backyard and her tail was covered in white paint. The dog had knocked the paint off the shelf.

Another afternoon I got home before the others and again he was drunk. I tried to get to the safety of my room, but he caught me. He said he wanted to try something. He wanted to hypnotize me.

He'd seen it done somewhere and wanted to try it. He had me sit in a chair and dangled a locket in front of my face. He said, "keep your eyes on the locket," as it swayed back and forth, "You're getting sleepy." Out of sheer terror I pretended my eyes were getting heavy. When they were closed he said, "From now on when I say the words, 'Cara-madam', you will automatically go into a deep sleep." At this point, he pushed me back in the chair and unfastened my pants. He worked them down my legs and touched me in ways I should never have been touched.

I was afraid to say anything to my Mom about what happened. It continued. I remember one day in particular. I was twelve years old. I ran to the alley behind our house to see if his car was in the driveway. It was there. He was home. I snuck down the alley and sat on the curb at the end of our block, out of sight of our house. It was cold and raining. As I sat there shivering I started crying and questioned God. "How could you allow things like this to happen to little kids?" I blamed God for everything that was happening to me and I was angry.

It took forever to get the courage to tell our mom. When I finally did, she did nothing. She acted as if she didn't believe me.

He molested me for two years and I started running away from home. I hated this man and grew to hate my mom for not believing me, for not protecting me.

After four years in Illinois, we were transferred to Norfolk, Virginia. I made new friends and began to rebel. I smoked pot for the first time. Just knowing it was illegal was good enough for me.

My stepfather forced my brother and I to have military regulation haircuts in the past. That was over. I started letting my hair grow and tried other drugs.

He was stationed on a ship and I hoped he would be sent out to sea. One day he fell on the ship and broke his leg. I was glad to see him helpless and in pain.

The Navy sent him to work in a hospital because he couldn't get around his ship. He was assigned to help out in a pharmacy.

I was vacuuming their room one afternoon when no one was home and got a glimpse of a bunch of pill bottles on the top shelf of his closet. There were way too many bottles for it to have been from a prescription. He was stealing them, and never noticed the five bottles I took. Each contained 250, five-milligram Valium. At sixteen, this began my education in prescription drugs.

One Friday night I went camping with some friends and took forty-four yellow Valium, washing them down with warm beer. I got really sick and couldn't remember the next several days. Somehow, when I came to, I was staying with my girlfriend, Lois and her family.

Her Dad was also in the Navy but he was out at sea. I quit going to school altogether. Lois' Mom was very nice to me. I guess Lois told her about my stepfather.

They were building new houses in our subdivision. It was called Camelot and there was actually a man-made moat around it. I got a job with one of the builders as a laborer.

Lois' Mom made a sack lunch for me every morning. She was so sweet. She even put enough change in the bag for me to buy a soft drink. This went on for months and Lois' dad came home. Under the circumstances he was very nice.

One night after dinner he and I had a talk. He said I could stay until after Christmas but I needed to find another place to stay.

I waited for my stepfather to leave for work one morning and went to the house to talk to my mom. I told her I couldn't stay at Lois' any longer and the best thing I could do was join the Army. She signed the papers, and I went to basic training at Fort Knox, Kentucky.

I was a baby-faced, seventeen year old, younger than most in my company. It was January and extremely cold in the old wooden barracks. One night it snowed and there was a guy that kept everyone awake with his snoring. Six of us gently picked up his mattress, with him still on it, carried him down the stairs and left him in the snow. He never woke up. The sergeant found him still there the next morning.

We went on eight-mile force marches over hills called, "Heartbreak, Agony, and Misery," in the snow with an ambulance following our every step.

I landed in the hospital with frostbite and Rubella (German measles). It was very contagious and they put me in an isolation ward with thirteen others. The frostbite caused a layer of skin to peel off my feet and was extremely painful. Every now and then, my sergeant came by to check on me. During one of his visits he said if I missed too many days I would be recycled and have to start over. My company was qualifying on the rifle range.

After spending thirteen days in the hospital I was terrified of being recycled. When released, I qualified expert with the M-16 rifle.

I made it!

I had a little business card given to me by my recruiter that guaranteed I would be stationed in Hawaii, or, I could get out of the service.

I arrived at the Honolulu airport late at night. A pretty girl came up to me and placed a flower Lei around my neck. There was a military shuttle car waiting to take me to Schofield Barracks. After we drove out of the airport parking lot the driver took out a pipe and filled it with pot. He lit it and handed it back to me. I was wasted when we arrived. This became the norm.

I was assigned to a room I shared with three others. The room contained a desk and two bunk beds. Every night after work we sat around and smoked pot. This was not my plan. I wanted structure and discipline in my life. I thought I would get it by joining the Army.

After several months our unit, the 125th Signal Battalion, was transferred to Helemano Military Reservation. It was just past a little town called Wahiawa, towards the North Shore of Oahu. This barracks had two-man rooms. Every night we went room to room, and each had a different kind of pot.

There was a room at the end of the hallway I heard stories about. Something called cocaine, but I had no idea what it was. At the end of each night everyone seemed to disappear and I knew where they were. I tried to stay away and I did for several months. Then one night I knocked on the door. There were fifteen people in this room. I remember the look of surprise on their faces when they saw it was me.

I watched, as each guy took the belt and wrapped it around his arm. Someone inserted the needle into his vein and pumped the plunger of the syringe. I cringed as I watched in horror. I could never do that. I wanted to run as far and as fast as I could. I did. I couldn't believe people would take such chances.

Everything I heard about shooting dope was crazy!

One Friday night it was like I was in a trance. I knocked on that door. I'll never forget the look of pleasure I saw appear on each mans' face as the drug was shot into his vein. I wanted to feel what they were feeling and I asked for a turn.

Everyone in the room turned to look at me. Someone asked if I was sure and I said, yes. It was like something I could never have dreamed.

I am embarrassed and ashamed of what I did but it's important you know the truth.

I got out of the Army and arrived at the Nashville Airport on March 26, 1975. It was twenty-six degrees outside. I sold my field jacket while in Hawaii. I didn't need it there but I could sure use it now.

I changed my plane ticket home in order to stop in Nashville and visit my grandparents.

2 SAFE HAVEN

Our stepfather and mother allowed us kids to spend a few summers with our grandparents in Nashville, Tennessee. They were very hardworking people.

Granddaddy worked for Genesco making shoes for forty-four years. My grandmother worked for the state of Tennessee. They had a summer cottage with a boat dock on Old Hickory Lake. That's where we stayed when we visited.

Granddaddy taught us to fish. He had a small aluminum boat with a 25-horsepower Evinrude motor. We made our own trotlines and seined a section of Whites Creek for minnows and crawdads to use as bait.

My favorite thing was to use top water lures and fish for bass. We didn't need a trolling motor;

Granddaddy paddled, and got great pleasure just watching me fish. After fishing, we returned to the cottage and he cooked country ham and redeye gravy.

We called our grandmother, Murr. She made the best biscuits and homemade strawberry jam. Well, it was difficult to choose, between her blackberry and strawberry jam. There was a blackberry patch just down the road from the cottage.

Granddaddy took me to hunt for sassafras root. Murr liked to keep some simmering in a pan on the stove for the incredible smell. We made homemade ice cream and spent what time we weren't fishing, swimming and getting a great tan. My favorite song was, "In The Summertime," by Mungo Jerry.

It was our getaway. We were blessed to have such wonderful grandparents.

I recognized their car as they pulled to the curb to pick me up. I explained why I didn't have a coat. Murr said, "We'll take care of that."

We had a great visit. I secretly told my grandmother what my stepfather had done. She said, "You can't go back there, you're going to stay with us until you get on your feet. I have a little money put away for you to go to school."

I enrolled in computer programming classes at Nashville State Technical Institute and found a part time job. A short time later, Granddaddy was diagnosed with lung cancer. It was a terrible time. He eventually had surgery on his brain that left him paralyzed on his right side. He couldn't speak.

Murr took care of him all day. When I got home in the evening I would pick him up from his recliner and carry him to the hospital bed in his room.

One night I was saying goodnight to Granddaddy, and as I held his hand he squeezed extremely hard. I noticed but thought nothing of it.

The next morning I woke to the sound of Aunt Pat's voice. I knew something was wrong for her to be there that early. Granddaddy passed away during the night. He knew he was dying. That's why he squeezed my hand so hard. He was telling me to take care of my grandmother.

3 FINDING PURPOSE

I couldn't keep my mind on studies and quit school. I found a full-time job at Baird Ward Printing Company. I stood at the end of a printing press and stacked pages on a wooden palette for twelve hours at a time. I worked there five years and met a guy whose father was a construction superintendent. He eventually quit the printing company and went to work with his dad.

He called me one day and asked if I wanted a job, I said, "Yes." We did all types of carpentry but mainly we poured a lot of concrete.

I worked with them for years. It wasn't fulfilling. I wanted to do something different. I was working for American Constructors on an extremely large church, Christ Church, on Old Hickory Blvd., in

Nashville. It was a brutally cold winter. One morning I was working near two electricians and they were talking about 'the big house.' I knew that was the penitentiary. These guys had been cellmates in prison. I listened to their conversation as lunch time approached. When I went to lunch I stopped at the portable john. I was coming out and noticed a syringe lying in the gravel. Someone had been in there shooting dope. It brought back memories of my time in the Army. I asked myself, 'If I could be anything in the world, what would I be?' Out of the blue came, 'I want to be a photographer.'

I investigated and found that Nashville State Technical Institute had a one-year certificate course in photography. I enrolled and started night classes. I also bought the kind of camera a professional photographer would use, a Nikon F3hp.

It was incredibly difficult working construction all day and going to school at night. It took me almost two years to finish the one-year certificate course.

One night I stayed up all night worrying about the direction my life was taking. I went to work and told my superintendent, Wade Brown, I appreciated the opportunity he'd given me but I wanted to do something else.

He stood up from behind his desk and shook my hand. "Mike, there is nothing to thank me for. You earned everything you got here, good luck," he said.

I found out just how difficult it was to find work in photography. I actually worked two weeks free for Mr. Kuffrey at his small studio on Nolensville Road. He must have thought I was crazy. He was an older gentleman basically surviving on copy work. People brought in pictures they wanted copied, and he performed the service.

The first week he taught me the process. I was doing all the orders as he sat and talked to a friend of his. I even ran errands for him.

I eventually found a job at Capitol One Hour Photo, in Franklin, Tennessee. I embraced the job and became as good as I could at printing people's vacation pictures. Most of the pictures were horrible, but it was fun.

One day while reading the classified section of the local newspaper I noticed a job opening for a photographer. I gave in to fear and put the thought out of my head for several days. On the third day I called. Ron Taylor, the managing editor of the Review Appeal Newspaper said he filled the position that morning. He also said I could bring in my portfolio and if anything came open he would consider me. I did the next day.

Two days later, Ron called and said, "I need someone to run the darkroom, but the job only pays $4.50 an hour. Would you be interested?" I said, "Yes."

The photographer he hired worked two days and quit. Ron cropped his picture of a lady gardening in such a manner that when the picture published she had no hands. The picture did look stupid in the paper. Ron came back to the darkroom and said, "I told you if a position came open I would consider you, do you want the photographer job?"

"Yes," I said.

My very first paid assignment was to photograph a bunch of children picking pumpkins at Clint Callicott's farm in Franklin, Tennessee for Halloween 1988.

The newspaper did not replace me as a darkroom tech. I did it all. I created a photography department and fell in love with Williamson County and the people. Most of all, I fell in love with photojournalism. Telling stories with pictures.

I went to photography seminars and joined the National Press Photographers Association. I read every magazine and book I could find about newspaper photography. Every year the NPPA sent me a book titled, "The Best of Photojournalism." Wow! The pictures took my breath away.

I bought a scanner and learned all the codes the police, fire, and rescue squad used. I slept with it on my headboard. For the next eight years, I ate, slept, and breathed newspaper photography.

One year, I won two first place awards and a second place in the annual University of Tennessee Press Association Awards. There were only three categories at that time, best news photo, best feature photo and best sports photo. Hugh Dupree was the publisher and he wanted to do something different this year. The publisher usually went to the banquet and collected the awards the newspaper won. Hugh decided the people that actually won the awards could go receive them in person.

The banquet was held in Memphis and we were put up at the Peabody Hotel. It's very famous for the family of ducks that are treated like royalty. At the appointed hour they are brought down in the elevator and walk a red carpet to the fountain in the lobby. The first day I saw the ducks and walked down to Beale Street for some really great blues music.

The next morning was Saturday and we all took off to Graceland. The Tennessee Press Association reserved it for the day. I'm not the most avid Elvis fan but Graceland was fantastic.

I was eventually allowed to hire a darkroom tech to process film while I was out taking pictures.

Then it happened. I had a shooting pain in my neck that would not stop. After suffering for several weeks I went to the doctor and was told I needed neurosurgery. I slipped two cervical disks. It was a relief to find a solution for the incredible pain. My health insurance was covering all the medical bills. I went to the publisher and said, "It's not right for my insurance to cover my medical bills. My injury was caused by carrying the heavy camera bag for eight years." He had me fill out an injury report and the newspaper decided to fight my claim.

My doctor sent a letter to my caseworker, Ken Palumbo, at the Tennessee Department of Labor, Division of Workers' Comp stating he knew my injury was work related. This caused Palumbo to issue a court order forcing Morris Newspaper Corporation to pay my medical bills and benefits. Morris filed a lawsuit against me to recoup those expenses. I spent the next six months recuperating and eventually quit my job at the newspaper.

The Review Appeal would not let me return to taking pictures. A year after the injury I went to court against Morris Newspaper Corporation and lost the case. The unbelievable part, Ken Palumbo was now an employee of Morris Newspaper Corporation and was with their lawyers in the courtroom. The letter from my doctor was not thrown out under the pretext that he wrote it out of sympathy for me.

The judge said the 10% permanent disability that resulted from my surgery would keep me from ever taking pictures again. I begged to differ.

Since the Tennessee Division of Worker's Compensation issued a court order in my case, the end result was the state of Tennessee would now have to pay all my medical bills. Before it was over I won fourteen University Of Tennessee Press Awards for the Review Appeal Newspaper.

4 AFTER THE REVIEW APPEAL NEWSPAPER

I moved in with my grandmother and realized she should not be living alone any longer at 88 years old. She wasn't eating right or taking care of herself.

The friend whose father was a construction superintendent, well, I called him and was again working construction. It was humbling to go back.

I found a little restaurant we in the south call, 'a meat n three where I could get dinner for my grandmother and I. Every evening I did just that.

One afternoon I stopped at a McDonald's restaurant a mile from granny's house. There were orange cones and caution tape roping off recent damage to the building. Someone drove a car through the front plate glass window and the car came to rest inside the building. No one was injured. The cashier told me about a little old lady that comes in every Sunday morning at 7 a.m. sharp. She buys coffee, sits in the corner, and reads her paper. Forty-five minutes later, she leaves for the 8 a.m. service at the Madison Church of Christ across the street. The cashier said, "I heard the engine revving and this big old boat of a car jumped the curb and came crashing through the window. She thought it was in reverse, but it wasn't"

"What color was the car?" I asked. "Brown," she replied, the same color as granny's Caprice. I looked at my watch and it was Thursday. Granny was getting her hair done right now only blocks away. I drove over and saw her car in the parking lot of the hair salon. There was visible damage on the hood. I crossed my arms and leaned against her fender. She was shocked to see me waiting and I gave her a big hug. "I'm sure glad you weren't hurt when you drove through the McDonald's Restaurant," I said. I drove her home and took her keys. That was the last time granny drove.

The bill for the damage was $18,000. The state of Tennessee took her drivers' license.

After two years of living with my grandmother I went out one night and met a woman from Lexington, Kentucky. We became very close and spent hours on the phone. Her sister lived in Nashville and she visited every chance she got.

I called my sister and told her I wanted to move to Lexington, Kentucky and try to work for The Lexington Herald Newspaper as a photographer. I wasn't having any luck getting work at The Tennessean Newspaper.

She said I'd taken care of Murr long enough it was her turn. She was going to come get her and take her to live in Norfolk.

I moved to Lexington and interviewed at the newspaper. The photo editor liked my work and I signed a freelance agreement. I was very excited, but the only call I received from the photo editor was a message telling me to be patient, they really were planning on using me. Six months went by and I didn't receive any more calls. In the meantime, I found work as carpenter.

The relationship fizzled out and I wanted to go home. I called Murr in Norfolk and she was excited I wanted to return to Nashville and said, "If you do please take care of my house."

On a rainy Friday night I loaded my furniture in a U-Haul truck and drove home. I opened the back door to my grandmother's house and the smell of mothballs took my breath away. Granny lived in this house for fifty years. My sister put most of her furniture in storage and left just enough to make the house look lived in.

I propped the door open in the cold winter air and went frantically through the house searching for the source of the smell. There were mothballs everywhere. Tears were streaming down my face, I ran outside for fresh air.

I decided to make repairs to the house to earn my keep. She'd closed off most of the house to save on the electric bill. The walls, and even the furniture of the closed off rooms, had mold on them.

I had most of the tools I needed and bought the necessary supplies. I worked into the winter sanding and repairing cracks in the walls. I gently removed the shoe mold and wood baseboard and stripped the finish by hand.

I pulled a section of the textured green carpet back and there were solid oak floors underneath. They were in pretty bad shape but that could be fixed. Each room took three coats of paint and the house was really beginning to look great.

One day I impulsively picked up the phone and dialed the number for the Tennessean Newspaper. I asked to speak to the photo editor. I'd done this many times before. This time was different. Randy Piland was not the photo editor anymore. Tom Stanford answered the phone. "Could I show you my portfolio and maybe pick up some freelance work?" I asked.

He said, "I'll be glad to take a look at your pictures." We set a time for my visit.

It was an amazing feeling after all the years of trying to finally walk into the Tennessean building carrying my portfolio. I was greeted at the reception area and told the young lady I was there to see Tom Stanford.

We shook hands and I followed him through the building to the photo desk. He sat down and I handed him my portfolio which consisted of about 20, 8 x 10 black and white prints. When he was through, he looked up at me and said, "You'll have to sign a freelance agreement to shoot for us."

"I'd be happy to," I said.

I couldn't believe it. He went to get a contract for me to sign, and as I waited, Lisa Nipp came to the photo desk. She was a great photographer. I was excited to see her. During my eight years at the small newspaper in Franklin I met most of the Tennessean photographers. Whenever I was on assignment and saw someone with professional looking photo gear I introduced myself.

I told Lisa, "Tom is getting me a freelance agreement to sign." She seemed excited for me. "To me, it's like a minor league baseball player coming to the show," I said. I always wanted to shoot in the big leagues. After signing the agreement, I left the building fighting back tears of joy. The Tennessean was the 57th largest newspaper in the country.

My friend, Eddie, came over and helped me drag the rolls of carpet out to a U-Haul truck so we could take them to the dump. I rented a floor sander from Lowe's and began restoring the oak floors. I continued to work into the night and found myself going to sleep as the sun came up.

After months of waiting, the phone finally rang. "Tom Stanford. Can you shoot an assignment for us?" the voice said. "Absolutely!!!" I responded. "I need you to go to the Tennessee Titans training facility and photograph running back Eddie George during practice," he said.

When I signed the contract, Tom gave me four rolls of film. I got some pretty good shots and they were published.

Wow! The assignments were very slow to come in the beginning but I was blessed with a couple of great opportunities. One morning my pictures were the lead on three of the papers' section fronts.

My confidence as a shooter was coming back and the staffers at the Tennessean were great to be around. They were incredible photographers. To me, these people were legends. I could almost tell who shot what picture just by looking at the style of the photograph.

5 SERPENT HANDLING

One morning after working late into the night, the phone rang.

"Can you cover an assignment in East Tennessee? There's been a mix-up in the daily assignments. The reporter is already on his way. The story is about churches that handle snakes. Head east on I-40 and call when you need gas, I'll be able to tell you more then," Tom said.

"I have a full tank of gas," I replied. "I can drive four hours on a full tank." "Call me when you need gas," he said and hung up.

Just outside Knoxville, I stopped and called the newspaper. Nina Long was working the photo desk and she said, "Tom is in a meeting. All I can tell you is your assignment is in Parrottsville, Tennessee.

You are going to the home of John and Peggy Brown. I don't have an address, that's all I know."

I found Parrottsville on my map. It was 45 minutes away. There wasn't even a traffic signal. I stopped at a market, and asked the clerk if I could borrow a phone book. I found a listing for John and Peggy Brown. But the address was not on any of the maps in the back. I asked the clerk if she knew where Cottage Way was. A gentleman in line behind me said, "I know that address. I'm a volunteer fireman and we've had calls out there."

He offered to show me if I would follow him. After several miles we turned onto a gravel road and the gentleman's truck came to a stop. I pulled next to him and he said he would point to the house as he drove by but he would not stop.

"They are serpent-handlers, I'll turn around in a driveway down the road. I know the folks that live there," he said.

I pulled into the driveway as he pointed and I waved, thank you. I parked behind a mini-van with Davidson County tags (Nashville) and got out of my 1988 Grand Am with my heart racing. At least the reporter is here.

I approached the small one story home with a magnificent view of the surrounding hills. A woman came out the front door and greeted me with a warm smile. She introduced herself as Peggy Brown. She reminded me of my Aunt Matti.

She invited me in and said, "Mike is already here." I was relieved to see Mike Kilen sitting on the couch. He arrived twenty minutes before me. Wow, I almost caught up with him and didn't even know where I was going.

The walls of John and Peggy's living room were adorned with pictures. I continued to look around and noticed a photograph of someone holding a rattlesnake!

"John will be home in a little while. He's still working. John's a carpenter," Peggy said.

Mike talked to Peggy and I listened to find out what the story was about. In 1995, Peggy's daughter-in-law, Melinda, was bit by a black timber rattlesnake during services at the Full Gospel Tabernacle In Jesus Name in Middlesboro, Kentucky. She passed away from the bite.

Three years later Peggy's son, John Wayne Punkin Brown, Melinda's husband, was bitten during a service at the Rock House Holiness Church in Macedonia, Alabama and died within fifteen minutes. His death left their five children orphans.

The story we were sent to cover was regarding a custody battle for their children. Both sets of grandparents vying for custody, had at one time taken up serpents.

I heard a car door shut. My heart raced as the screen door creaked open and I saw John Brown appear in the doorway. "How ya'll doin?" he said, making eye contact with each of us. We stood shook his hand and introduced ourselves.

He made his way to his recliner. I looked at the picture of he and Peggy over the entryway to the kitchen. It must have been taken at least twenty years earlier.

Mike and John talked about the custody battle and the hearings. John expressed his doubt as to the motivation of the other grandparents. "They want the Social Security money," he said.

"Why do you handle serpents?" Mike asked. "I do it because the Bible says to do it." He fumbled through his pockets and shouted, "Peggy, where are my glasses?"

Peggy brought John his glasses as he opened his King James Bible. He read aloud,

"Mark 16:17-18: And these signs shall follow them that believe; In my name shall they cast out devils; they shall speak with new tongues; they shall take up serpents; and if they drink any deadly thing, it shall not hurt them; they shall lay hands on the sick and they shall recover."

John read with conviction and the rhythm of what I would come to know as a "serpent handling" preacher.

With John it was always quid pro quo. He wanted something in return. He asked each of us about our beliefs. Mike was Catholic and I was Christian. I had not been baptized and I didn't attend church. Peggy brought John a cup of coffee.

"We are not a cult and we don't worship snakes," Peggy said as she walked into the kitchen. We visited for another hour and as we left John invited us to a service at his church the following Saturday night. We thanked them for their hospitality and said our goodbyes.

Mike and I met Saturday morning at a Cracker Barrel Restaurant and he rode with me the three and a half hours to the Browns' home. We shared our anxiety and our expectations of the church service as we made the drive.

Mike said, "Our initial visit to the Brown home was the result of many, many messages left on their answering machine. Their motivation in returning my call was hope publicity would help them in their custody battle for the grandchildren."

We arrived and were greeted warmly by John and Peggy. She smiled that same warm smile I saw on my first visit. We sat in the living room as John finished getting ready for church.

"Mike, when John found God I was so glad because before he would go to sleep with a glass of whiskey beside the bed. He would wake up in the middle of the night and need a drink. After he found God that went away. Sometimes, serpents are taken up and sometimes they're not. It's all in if the Lord moves. John hasn't taken up a serpent in months."

Would tonight be the night serpents were taken up? I tried to keep up with John's Pontiac speeding through the hills of East Tennessee.

His church was just over the Tennessee-North Carolina border in Marshall, North Carolina. It was a little over an hour drive. We hit speeds of 75 mph, much too fast for the two lane road winding through the Pisgah National Forest. We passed a little country grocery store called, "Murr's." The anticipation was overwhelming as we neared the tiny white church on the side of a mountain.

"No one has photographed in my church in twenty-five years and I see no reason to start now. You're welcome to worship the Lord but leave your cameras and tape recorders in the car," John said.

Chills came over me as I noticed two headstones down a path to the right of the church entrance. We entered and John introduced us to Mark Brown John's youngest son, and Steve Frazier John's nephew.

Mike and I sat in the last pew on the left and waited for the service to begin. He placed a small tape recorder on the wooden bench next to him. I was concerned someone would see it and say something.

The women wore long dresses and no makeup. Peggy Brown's hair was so long it flowed down the back of her legs.

The men wore pressed long sleeve shirts and jeans. No ties or suits in this crowd. Several men entered the church carrying flat wooden boxes some displaying many coats of varnish. The boxes were placed on the floor behind the altar.

A glass of clear liquid, a Bible open to Mark 16:17-18, and a bottle of olive oil were on the altar.

Mike Kilen and I looked at each other. I was overcome with an intense desire to raise my feet off the floor as the service started with the eruption of symbol thumping, guitar strumming and an electric keyboard. John held his hands up high, closed his eyes and exclaimed, "Praise God!" Song after song built up a rhythm to the service. The music stopped.

"There's death in them boxes for them that take a serpent up without the anointing. Wait until the Lord moves!" John preached.

He grabbed the bottle of olive oil and poured some in his hand. After rubbing his hands together he approached a man sitting on the pew along the wall.

He held one hand on the man's forehead and with the other hand raised he closed his eyes and spoke a language unknown to man. One by one members of the congregation approached to receive a healing touch from John, the Pastor and Patriarch of this congregation. He began to preach his sermon at a fever pitch. The following is an excerpt from Mike Kilen's story:

"Today I'm talkin' to you about salvation! Amen ... You'll not escape the judgment of Gawd!... Amen...death has no age limit; My son was 34 year old...Amen... I don't care how pretty you are or how ugly you are...Amen... death has been on our trail since we were born into this world...Amen...Today could be your day!"

John disappeared kneeling behind the altar. A moment passed then all of a sudden he stands up holding a huge rattlesnake.

The women in the church exclaim, "Jesus! Jesus!" They rise hands held high. Speaking in tongues overtakes the congregation, shouting and thumping of symbols. The Lord has moved.

John skips around the altar holding the snake eighteen inches from its' deadly head. He is sweating profusely. As he turns to face the serpent and he sticks his tongue out. A moment that seems to last forever passes and the serpent sticks its' tongue out at John.

Victory!

John made his way behind the altar and placed the serpent back into the box. He stood and wiped his face with a handkerchief as he recognized the visitors before the congregation.

One by one each person stood and thanked God for the blessings in their lives. My turn approached and I couldn't stop shaking. Mike's turn came first but I didn't hear a word he said. All of a sudden everyone was looking at me. I stood and thanked God for the blessings in my life. The service came to a close and Mike slid his recorder into his pocket.

We made our way to the parking lot. I asked John and Peggy, "Could I please take a picture of the two of you with the church in the background?" John looked at Peggy and nodded, "Ok." I wasn't allowed to photograph a service but I had art to lead the story. Mike and I drove home and expressed our emotions at what we'd just witnessed. Wow!

The story published in the Tennessean with my portrait of John and Peggy as the lead. An incredible photograph taken by an Associated Press photographer of John Wayne Punkin Brown holding a rattlesnake ran as part of the package.

John Wayne Punkin Brown was an outspoken evangelist in the faith and indiscriminately allowed photographers to photograph him during services at other churches. As for John Brown Sr., photos of him taking up serpents had been used against him in the custody battle for his grandchildren.

Mike Kilen achieved his goal and wrote a great story. The experience was over for him. For me, it was just beginning. I had to photograph this phenomenon. How often do you have an opportunity to photograph faith?

I searched for all the information I could find about serpent handling. Two books captured my attention, "Faith, Serpents and Fire," by Scott Schwartz, and Dr. Thomas Burtons' book, "Serpent-Handling Believers." The latter had a picture of a beautiful young Minnie Parker with a rattlesnake stretched across her brow, unbelievable. It was taken in 1947 at the Dolley Pond Church of God With Signs Following near Chattanooga, Tennessee. I also bought a book about rattlesnakes. I needed to know everything I could about rattlesnakes.

One afternoon I drove to East Tennessee State University and searched the collection called, "The Archives of Appalachia." I watched videotaped interviews of famous serpent-handling ministers. The one that stood out from the rest was an interview with Charles Prince. A picture of Prince holding two rattlesnakes in one hand is on the cover of Dr. Burton's book.

The one thing that impressed me was the compassion Dr. Burton and Scott Schwartz obviously felt for these people. Everyone I talked to about serpent handling said they were crazy, and I was crazy for going to visit.

If the first time I met John Brown was in his church taking up a serpent I might have felt differently about him. But I met him at his home and he seemed like a very kind humble hardworking family man.

I did a little research and found out the two graves just outside the entrance to John's church were Buford Pack and Jimmy Ray Williams. The two young men died after drinking strychnine during a service at the Holiness Church of God In Jesus Name Church in Carson Springs, Tennessee. The graves had been moved to John's church after the Carson Spring's church closed down.

The final ruling in the custody battle declared John and Peggy must share custody with the other grandparents and the grandchildren could not be in church if serpents were there.

John was following the court order and it hurt him with his congregation. They were supposed to follow God's law not mans. Attendance dwindled.

After each visit to John's church I followed them home and we talked about everything. It was apparent he wanted to bring me to God and to John that meant me taking up a serpent. I don't think so. I was terrified of snakes. It was a dangerous game I was playing but I desperately wanted pictures of a service. John teased me with statements like, "It's not up to me. I have to discuss it with the elders of my church."

Teasing back I went as far as calling John and Peggy, "Brother John, and Sister Peggy." I knew I was crossing the line.

During one of our talks John said, "To be saved you must forgive all that have sinned against you. Not only that but you must pray they too would come to know Jesus Christ as their Savior."

Well, I knew that wasn't going to happen because I could not forgive my stepfather for what he had done.

While visiting one day I asked John about Pastor Jimmy Morrow. John talked about him a lot and I asked if we could go to a service at his church. "Sure," John said.

He took me to visit Pastor Morrow at his home before the service. His wife, Pam, was so shy it was all she could do to peek around the doorway. Pastor Morrow pulled out a collection of newspaper clippings. Every article was about serpent handling. He had a definite fascination with the history of it and we spent two hours looking through everything.

It was time for the church service. John and I rode together to the Edwina Church of God In Jesus Christ Name in Newport, Tennessee. We walked in and John motioned for me to sit down. The pew was turned against the wall in front of the rest of the congregation. I guessed from being in John's church this pew was used for visiting dignitaries and it was very possible serpent handling could be going on very close. I started to sweat and got very anxious. I asked for this. I asked John to bring me here. What was I expecting? John got up and went to talk to Pastor Morrow. The minute I realized the coast was clear I slid down the pew. I wanted more distance between me and someone with a rattlesnake. I took John's spot! He came back and gave me the funniest look.

The service began with music and Pastor Morrow preaching. They had the same instruments as John's church, symbols, guitar and a keyboard. People streamed in and the crowd grew. Pastor Morrow got out a copperhead as another man held a big timber rattlesnake. They danced to the rhythm of the music and spoke in tongues. I saw a woman hold her hand over a candle flame but didn't appear to feel pain from it. I also saw Pastor Morrow's wife, Pam, take up a copperhead. I was a little too close to the action for comfort. John didn't take up a serpent that night and I was relieved.

I remained persistent wanting to photograph a service and John kept after me to come to terms with forgiveness. The three and a half hour drive from the Browns' home to mine always gave me plenty of time to reflect on my last visit.

One night, after another late night talk with John, he stepped out on his back porch to see me off. He asked, "Do you have enough money for gas to get home? Can I make a sandwich for you to eat on the drive?"

"No John, thank you I'm alright." I said.

I was an hour into my drive and started thinking about how kind he had been. Offering to give me money. He treated me like a father would treat his son. Out of nowhere I started crying and praying for my stepfather. I had to pull off the interstate I was crying so hard. On Interstate 40 somewhere between Knoxville and Nashville, at two-thirty in the morning, I found forgiveness in my heart and dedicated my life to my Lord and Savior Jesus Christ.

I prayed, "Lord, I have made a complete mess of my life. Please use me as you see fit." I sat back in my seat and a calm like I have never known came over me. Over the next several weeks I wanted to visit the Browns and share what happened but I needed to work.

I was broke.

6 GRANNY'S SURGERY

My sister, Trish, called and said, "Murr has fallen and shattered her hip. The doctor said because of her age he would not advise operating on her. He doubted whether she would survive the surgery. Make her as comfortable as you can, she has six months."

Trish found a doctor that performed a complete hip replacement on someone older than Granny and they had done well. He agreed to perform her surgery and a date was set. The odds the doctor gave she would survive the surgery were, 50-50.

We were allowed to wait in her room for her to come from recovery. Finally, the doctor came in and explained there were no complications everything appeared fine. They brought her in and moved her to the hospital bed. We waited for her to wake. She did, an hour later, with an agonizing scream. She was in so much pain I couldn't bear it. We bothered the nurse for more pain medication but she said they had to let the medication from the surgery wear off before she could have anything. The next two days were terrible. The third day her pain started to subside. I told my sister I needed to work. I would have to leave in the morning. I kissed my grandmother and said goodbye.

I noticed white smoke trailing behind me and knew my car was on its last leg as I arrived in Nashville. Great, I can't work without a car. Sure enough the diagnosis was a blown head gasket. The engine had already been rebuilt several times. I didn't know what I was going to do. I got out my Hanes Repair Manual and studied what would have to be done to completely rebuild the engine. I would definitely save money doing the work myself. In the meantime I drove the 1974 Caprice my grandmother left in the driveway. It didn't take long to realize there was no guarantee I would arrive at my destination in her car. I began working on my car around the clock and thought it best to tell Tom I was temporarily out of commission. I didn't want to take an assignment and end up broke down on the side of the road. My friend, Eddie, helped me take the engine out of my car. I'd never rebuilt an engine and had my doubts to whether it would even start when completed. The third week in July I finished the job. It started but I couldn't control the idle. The engine sounded like it was going to blow up. I turned the key off before the tachometer red lined. It turned out to be a sensor and I had it fixed the next day. The engine ran great.

I called the Tennessean and started to get work again. Somehow I was going to get through this, by the Grace of God.

The inside of the house was finished and the three coats of polyurethane on the freshly sanded and stained floors made them shine like new money. What bothered me now were the three layers of shingles on the roof. Three layers are too much.

Tearing it off and putting a new roof on the house would go a long way to increase the value. My sister and I discussed the restoration every step of the way. The last time we talked she said, "If all you have left to do is the roof, it's time to think about selling the house." "I'll have a yard sale and hopefully make enough money to fix the roof," I said. She agreed.

7 THE ASSIGNMENT

August 16th, I started cleaning out the shed for the yard sale. The phone rang. I'd left the cordless phone on the picnic table and ran to answer it. Out of breath I answered. "Hello."

"My name is Kevin Eans, I'm a photo editor for USA Today. Tom Stanford recommended you and gave me your number. Can you shoot an assignment for me on Thursday?

"Absolutely." I replied.

"It's $225 a day, plus film, and 23 cents a mile," he said.

"The assignment is to photograph a surgery at Vanderbilt University Medical Center. It's a groundbreaking procedure on a child in utero. Bob Davis is the reporter and he'll be staying at the

Loews. Here's his cell number if you need to talk to him is --------."

I hung up the phone.

Thursday, August 19, 1999, would not be an ordinary day. The surgical procedure was to correct the medical condition of spina bifida on a fetus in its' twenty-first week of pregnancy.

I arrived at Vanderbilt University Medical Center at 9:15 a.m., fifteen minutes before my scheduled appointment. I waited in the lobby and saw John Howser as he came down the stairs. He is the Director of News & Communications and Media Relations at Vanderbilt. We exchanged greetings and he led me to a waiting room near the surgical suite. John explained he had been a newspaper photographer for ten years before going into public relations. We talked about photography and he told me about the time he met James Nachtwey, a very famous newspaper photographer.

As John and I sat in the waiting room a man entered. John introduced him as Robert Davis the reporter from USA Today that would be writing the story.

Robert explained, "Alex and Julie Armas, initially didn't want to be in the article. Julie's sister said to her, 'Just think of all the people that will know about this surgery because you did the article.' They changed their mind about participating in the story but didn't want to be identified in photos. I just talked them into allowing us a few shots. Grab your gear and let's go find them."

We took off, almost running. Robert whispered, "That's them coming," and pointed to Alex and Julie, with Dr. Joseph Bruner, walking toward us down a long hallway. I started shooting.

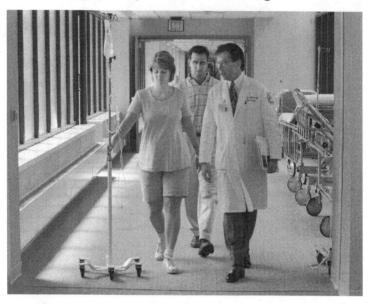

There was some paperwork for them to sign and Robert and I were allowed to be there. I got a few more shots.

Robert and I then met Dr. Noel Tulipan in his office. He is a pediatric neurosurgeon and does the actual repairs to the baby. He explained what spina bifida was and what would be done during the procedure. He showed us the most recent ultrasound images of the baby.

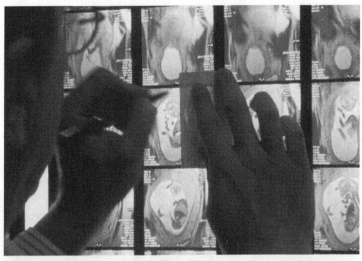

After returning to our waiting room John said to me, "We have a spot in the operating room for you to stand and you can't move from that spot. He left the room and returned several minutes later with two sets of surgical scrubs. He looked at me and said in a stern voice, "If I don't get these back they will cost you $8." He tossed a set to me. I got the point, he wanted them back.

John came to the door and asked Robert and I if we wanted lunch. I declined and he and Robert left for the cafeteria. I was afraid to eat anything. I'd never photographed a surgery before and I didn't want to get queasy.

A short time later Robert and John returned, "What did yall have?" I asked.

"Spaghetti," Robert replied.

"Sorry I asked," I said.

Great, now I'm in real trouble.

John entered the room and said, "Ready?" I grabbed my camera gear and we rushed to the operating room. This is a quote from Robert Davis' article:

"In the hushed but crowded operating room where outsiders were gathered to watch a rare medical event – spinal surgery on a fetus still in his mother's womb – a stool falls with a loud bang. "Shh," says Joseph Bruner, the surgeon leading the operation. "You'll wake the baby." Robert Davis continued, *"Waking the baby – or exciting the*

womb and causing the contractions associated with labor – would be fatal for the unborn child, Samuel Alexander Armas."

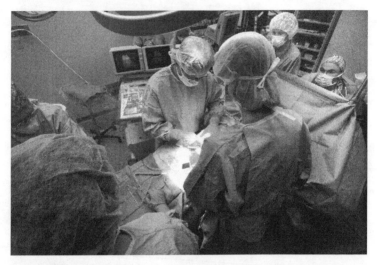

As I entered I greeted several of the medical personnel. A nurse asked me if I knew Deloris Delvin, another photographer at the paper and I acknowledged I did. She said, "She and I are friends."

The surgery was difficult to photograph because it was very graphic. Dr. Bruner performed a C-section bikini cut incision and lifted the uterus out. He then made an incision into the uterus. The amniotic fluid was removed and kept in a warming bath. I shot as much as I could with my wide-angle lens to make things look far away.

Dr. Bruner gently massaged the uterus to turn the baby to the correct position and the repairs were made.

I'd just changed to my Canon 85mm lens when Dr. Bruner made a comment and you could feel tension in the operating room lift. The critical part of the surgery was over.

Dr. Tulipan was standing to my left and asked, "What speed of film are you using?"

"800 Fuji", I responded. Out of the corner of my eye I saw the uterus shake, but no one was near it. It was shaking from within. Suddenly a tiny fist came flying through the surgical opening. Dr. Bruner and I made eye contact. He reacted and reached for the flailing little arm. Just before contact the child pulled back till only a tiny hand was exposed. The instant Dr. Bruner's finger made contact with the child's hand I pressed my camera's shutter button and held it down. I watched as the child squeezed the doctor's finger. I was able to captured four frames before I was grabbed from behind and literally picked up in the air. This person carried me several steps as he said, "You can get a better shot over here." When he put me down I desperately wanted to turn and see who grabbed me but I had to look for the baby's hand.

"Do it again! Do it again!" I said.

It happened so fast, a nurse asked, "What happened?"

"The child reached out," I said.

"Oh, they do that all the time," she responded.

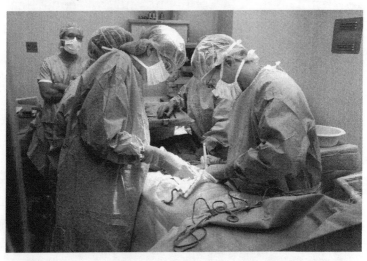

The doctors replaced the amniotic fluid and finished closing the surgical opening to the uterus. I felt very threatened by what just happened. I looked toward the door of the surgical suite and saw John Howser enter. A member of the medical staff approached him and whispered in his ear.

I looked at him and in an act of defiance held my arms out at my sides and yelled, "What the hell, John!" I was angry. Someone physically tried to stop me from capturing a picture of the baby's hand.

I followed Robert Davis and Dr. Bruner out of the OR and standing in the hallway was Alex Armas. His face was white as a sheet as he waited for word from Dr. Bruner about how the surgery had gone.

Dr. Bruner walked up to Alex and turned to look at me as he said, "I had a little fun with the photographer. I posed a picture for him." Alex had a confused, almost angry look come across his face. He looked at me and I said, "It happened so fast I can't be sure the picture will even be in focus."

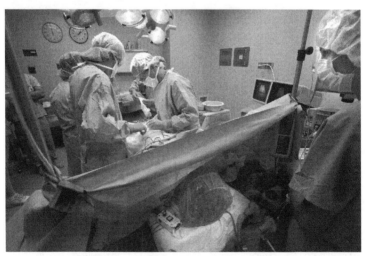

Robert Davis came up to me and said, "If the picture does come out you will be responsible for getting copies to the family because you retain all rights to the pictures."

I turned to Alex and asked, "Does the baby have a name?"

"Samuel Alexander Armas," he responded. I wrote it down in my notebook.

Kevin Eans, the USA Today Photo Editor, requested I FED-EX my unprocessed film to their lab immediately following the surgery. I said my goodbyes and walked to my car looking over my shoulder all the way. If someone from the medical staff was bold enough to physically grab me during the surgery how far would they go to stop the publication of the picture?

I drove across town to the FED-EX location and wrote a note, "Look for the hand picture, the baby's name is Samuel." I placed it in the envelope with the film and sealed the package.

The following day was Friday and I was back working for the Tennessean Newspaper. After my assignments I went to the photo desk, and talked to Sam Parrish, the night photo editor. "You're not going to believe what happened. Yesterday, I shot pictures of a surgery on an unborn child, for USA Today, and the child reached from the womb. But everything happened so fast I can't be sure the picture will even come out," I said. He looked at me with a puzzled look.

I waited to hear from USA Today about the assignment. Did the picture come out? Would they be happy with my work?

I waited as long as I could stand it and I called Kevin Eans. "Have you seen the film?" I asked.

"Not yet," he responded. "It sometimes takes a while."

It seemed like ten days passed and I called Kevin again. "It's the most incredible picture I've ever seen," he said.

Wow, it was in focus!

"We don't know when it will be published," he said. I was elated.

The yard sale was a tremendous success. Not only did I tear off the three layers of shingles, I replaced 1,500 board feet of lumber and re-did all the valleys. My brother, David, brought a co-worker and put the new shingles on in one day. Their ladder lift was broken and I hauled the seventy-five pound bundles of shingles up on the roof.

The house was finished.

One night while freelancing at the paper Sam called me and said, "Michael, I've got something you need to see."

I immediately got up and walked through the building to the photo desk. As I turned the corner I could see people gathered around Sam's computer. I got closer and saw the picture for the first time. Sam said, "That is a miraculous picture."

I couldn't believe it. The shutter speed of 1/60th of a second caused motion blur on the doctor's fingers, but the baby's hand was clearly in focus. Samuel squeezed tight enough, and long enough, to stop the action in the photograph.

Several days passed. Sam came up to me one night and asked, "If in fact you do retain all rights to the picture can we use it?" He was talking like a lawyer. His language puzzled me.

"Sure," I said. "I'd like something for it, maybe $50?"

"I think we could do that," he responded.

Frank Sutherland was the Executive Managing Editor of the Tennessean Newspaper at the time. One evening as I processed my film from the day's assignments I noticed Mr. Sutherland walk through the building and he never took his eyes off me. It was obvious he was looking straight at me. It happened three times in three hours. I had a very uneasy feeling.

Sam approached me the next day and said with a smirk, "You do in fact own all rights to this image."

Tom gave Kevin Eans, the USA Today photo editor, my phone number and Kevin called me directly. That meant I was shooting under USA Today's agreement which states, 'One time use only, photographer retains all rights.' My freelance agreement with the Tennessean states they retain all rights and if I shot the assignment for them they would own the picture.

USA Today and the Tennessean Newspaper are both part of the Gannett Newspaper chain.

The Tennessean obtained permission from Gannett Corporate to break the picture the same day USA Today published their story September 7, 1999.

Sam warned me, "You will have pro-lifers coming at you from every angle and you should be prepared."

I went in to the Tennessean one morning and someone said, "Cindy Smith gathered the entire night shift of reporters around a computer and said, 'I want you all to see a Pulitzer Prize photograph,' and showed them your picture."

The morning of September 7, 1999, I was at my grandmother's house and the phone rang. "Hello," I answered. "Mr. Clancy, I just want you to know your picture is already saving babies lives," the voice said. The gentleman identified himself as the manager of several pregnancy centers in the St. Louis area. I thanked him for the phone call and after hanging up I fell to my knees and cried uncontrollably. That was the first time I realized how powerful the picture was.

One week later I received an anonymous letter in the mail. It was a price list for body parts of aborted babies. A brain was listed for $999. I became furious. What sick person would send this to me? I tore it up and threw it away.

The next morning I passed Tom in the hallway and he said, "Just sold your baby's hand picture to Vanderbilt."

"You can't do that Tom," I said.

"You better check your agreement." He replied.

"Tom, I shot that assignment for USA Today, not you." I responded.

He thought for a minute and said, "You're right, I'll have to call Vanderbilt and tell them I erred in selling them rights to the picture."

The next several days everyone gave me advice about how I should manage the picture.

Nancy Rhoda, Features Photo Editor, recommended I call Jack Corn. He was at one time the Photo Editor at the Tennessean. He went on to head the photojournalism program at Western Kentucky State University. He left Western to become the photo editor at the Chicago Tribune. My first year in photojournalism I attended a seminar in Jackson, Tennessee and Jack Corn was the speaker.

I called him and he recommended I call Marcel Saba at Saba Press. "I don't know him personally but many photographers say he is the best," Jack said. I didn't have the negatives from USA Today. I would have to wait.

I hoped John Howser from Vanderbilt would call and say something about the picture. I waited six or seven days after the initial publication and I called John myself. "What did you think of the picture?" I asked. "You nailed it. I hate to tell you this, but it's already been done," he said. "What are you talking about John?" I asked. "I'm in the middle of something I don't want to be in the middle of," he responded. "Life Magazine came to Vanderbilt and shot a very similar picture." He went on to say, "You'll do alright with your picture, but the Life Magazine picture is incredible. It's intended to be on the cover of the December 1999 issue. They want to show how far medical science progressed in the twentieth century, operating on children still in the womb."

"Their picture is posed, right?" I asked.

"Yes," he responded.

"How old is their baby?" I asked.

"Twenty-four weeks," he replied. He also stated, "Life Magazine will finish their project by photographing the birth of the baby in their picture."

"Life Magazine should use my picture because it's real and my baby is the youngest they would even consider for the surgery," I said.

John didn't respond. It was apparent he was not happy with me.

The following morning the phone rang and a woman identifying herself as Susan asked, "Dr. Bruner would like to know if it would be possible to receive a color slide of the picture for a seminar he is attending tomorrow?"

I told her I would check with my photo lab and call her back. It was expensive to have the order rushed, $150. I returned Susan's call, "I can get it done, but it will cost $150." She asked me to hold on. She came back to say, "Dr. Bruner isn't going to pay to have it done."

"I'm so sorry, I've offended Dr. Bruner, I just don't have the $150 to pay for it myself," I said.

Susan again left the phone and returned saying, "I just found out you scooped Life Magazine, he's not going to pay for anything."

8 THE RACE TO BE PUBLISHED

I spent the next several days thinking about my conversations with John Howser and Susan. I contacted Gamma Liason, and spoke to Brian Felber. I explained, "I have a picture that scoops the December cover of Life Magazine." He didn't understand.

I got frustrated and said, "Just get Life Magazine on the phone and show them the picture, you won't have to say anything."

A friend emailed a small file of the picture to Brian for me. A short time later he called back and said, "Life Magazine does want to buy your picture. They want to buy it, to kill it."

My response was, "Bad choice of words, there isn't enough money in the world that would allow that to happen."

Life Magazine told Brian I could have overseas but not the U.S. When he said that I responded, "Who are they to say I can't market my picture in the U.S.?"

I asked Brian, "Who am I dealing with at Life Magazine?" He responded, "Vivette Porjes." Brian continued to negotiate with Life Magazine on my behalf.

On the second day of negotiations I decided it was time to tell them everything. I told Brian, "Tell them I know their picture is posed and I know their baby is twenty-four weeks. My baby is twenty-one weeks, the youngest they will consider for this surgery."

Brian must have had a phone to each ear because I could hear a woman screaming on the other line in response to that statement. "How does he know how old our baby is?"

I said to Brian, "If they don't use my picture I will find an agent to aggressively market my picture and by the time the December issue of Life Magazine is published the story will be old news."

At one point, I knew they were considering using my picture when Brian said, "They want to know what speed of film the picture is on?"

After the fourth day Brian called and said, "Negotiations went on late into the night, and were very heated at times, but Life Magazine decided to pass on your picture."

Now it was a race to have my picture published before the December issue of Life Magazine hit the street.

I took Jack Corn's advice and called Marcel Saba. I told him I had a photograph that scooped the December cover of Life Magazine. "Michael, this makes you look like a very shady character," he responded. I explained what happened and asked him to represent my photos. He agreed to manage the images.

Now it was time to fight for my picture. I wanted to enter it against the Life Magazine picture in all the major photography competitions. After all their picture was posed and mine was real. The most important photography contests are The Pulitzer Prize, World Press Photo, Pictures of the Year, and the competition for the Best in Magazine Photography, The Alfred Eisenstaedt Awards.

My picture's publication in newspapers already qualified it to be entered in World Press Photo, Pictures of the Year, and for a Pulitzer Prize. But to be entered for The Alfred Eisenstaedt Award the picture must be published in a major U.S. magazine before the end of the calendar year. It was nearing the end of September 1999. There were only two months left in the year.

Marcel Saba called and said, "A French magazine, VSD, is interested in publishing a page of pictures from the surgery. VSD is like People Magazine in the U.S."

"That's fantastic news," I said and pleaded with Marcel to approach U.S. magazines with the picture. Since Time and Life Magazines are affiliated I offered, "Please try Newsweek."

Marcel called several days later and said, "Good news Michael. Newsweek just purchased exclusive North American rights through November."

"Yes!!!!" I couldn't have been more excited. Marcel tried to explain why the use fee was so small, $2,000, but it didn't make sense to me. I was just learning about North American rights, International rights, exclusives, Internet rights, etc. I was sure glad to have Marcel to take care of all this.

I went to the bookstore every week in November to check the latest issue and there was no picture. Their exclusive had run out. Newsweek paid $2,000 and didn't publish it. Why would anyone throw away money like that?

I called Marcel and asked, "What happened? They didn't publish the picture."

His response, "What do you care, you got the money?"

I was heart broke. The picture was not published in a major U.S. magazine in 1999, and could not be entered in The Alfred Eisenstaedt Awards.

After the publication of the page of photos in the September/October issue of the French Magazine, VSD, the picture went into syndication and was published in newspapers and magazines throughout France, England, Scotland and Ireland.

The December 1999 issue of Life Magazine hit the bookstores and their picture was not on the cover. They buried their story, "Born Twice", in the last few pages of the issue.

If I had done my homework I would have known the Columbia University Graduate School of Journalism administers The Alfred Eisenstaedt Awards, under a grant from Life Magazine.

Max Aguilera-Hellweg's picture won first place in the science category and Marcel Saba was listed as a final judge in the competition. My picture couldn't be entered because it was not published in a major U.S. magazine in 1999.

Columbia University also awards The Pulitzer Prize.

Dr. Bruner had his first chance to speak publicly about Samuel's surgery and the photograph in an interview with the Tennessean Newspaper's Bill Snyder. Snyder's story, "The Picture That Went

Around The World," published January 9, 2000. In that interview Bruner denied Samuel reached out on his own. His quote was, "Depending on your political point of view, this is either Samuel Armas reaching out of the uterus and touching the finger of a fellow human, or it's me pulling his hand out of the uterus ... which is what I did."

When Tom Stanford at the Tennessean read Dr. Bruner's statement denying my claim that Samuel reached out on his own, he came to me and asked, "What's the truth?" I responded, "Dr. Bruner must be trying to get even with me for ruining his opportunity to be on the cover of Life Magazine."

I had the pictures, how could he possibly explain them away? I could see the look of relief on Tom Stanford's face now that the credibility of my picture had come into question. He was almost smiling. I was told he said during a staff meeting, "Why did Clancy get this picture?"

When I walked through the Tennessean I felt shrouded in a cloud of doubt. I received phone call after phone call from reporters, editors, of print and television media, from all over the world. They all asked me the same question, "Why is the doctor saying he posed the picture?"

They all seemed very disappointed. Everyone was calling Vanderbilt because it was the only reference in the cut line. John Howser told me his office was getting 20 calls a week for six months after the picture initially published.

Dr. Bruner and Vanderbilt suppressed a media firestorm, one phone call at a time.

9 SAMUEL IS BORN

I received a call from Alex Armas when Samuel was born on December 2, 1999. I asked if I could come visit and two days later drove to Atlanta. I brought extra copies of the picture for them. Seeing Samuel for the first time was overwhelming. He was beautiful. I wanted to take pictures but didn't feel comfortable enough to ask for permission. We visited for a little while and I drove back to Nashville.

Neither the Tennessean, nor USA Today, seemed interested in entering my picture for a Pulitzer Prize so I entered it myself. I also entered the Tennessean Newspaper for the Community Service Award for having the courage to publish the picture.

It cost me $50 for each entry and that was a huge expense for my extremely limited budget.

Jody from Saba Press called me early one morning and said my picture did not place in World Press, but took third place in the Pictures of the Year Competition.

It's only third place but attending the awards ceremony in Washington, D.C. would be a once in a lifetime event. I decided to attend.

Several days before my trip I received a phone call from a producer at MSNBC asking me to appear on their morning show to be interviewed about the picture. "I'll be in Washington that morning to accept an award for the picture," I said.

"Perfect," the producer said. "We'll send a car to pick you up and bring you to the studio."

It was very early in the morning when I arrived. I was told they contacted Dr. Bruner to be on the show and he initially agreed but called to back out at the last minute. I was put in a cold dark interview room with the Capitol Building in the background! I was nervous as a lady put a mic on me she said, "Try not to tap your feet."

I received a copy of the tape when it was over. I didn't realize at the time the segment was prefaced with a disclaimer explaining the doctor had a different version of the story.

That night was the awards ceremony. I had a feeling the controversy behind my picture would follow me and it did. I met Marcel Saba and Kevin Eans for the first time. I could tell when I looked Kevin in the eye he was excited to meet me and he knew my pictures were real. He had to have seen the four frames in the sequence and decided to only publish the one frame for their article.

I told Marcel I didn't want the picture in any of the tabloids like the National Enquirer, etc. I didn't want them making a mockery of it. Marcel called and said the three major tabloids wanted to publish the picture. At this point I reconsidered and felt any exposure would help tell my story. It published in the November 1999 issue of the National Enquirer. One of the emails I received told how Matt Drudge tried to show my picture, featured in the Enquirer, on his Fox television show. Network censors refused to allow him to show it. I'm embarrassed to say I didn't know who he was. I searched the web and there were many articles about the story. The dispute between Mr. Drudge and Fox censors ended his television career.

As I picked up my assignments for the next day, I noticed my first one was at Vanderbilt. I would see John Howser for the first time since Samuel's surgery. I couldn't sleep that night. John greeted me as I arrived for the assignment. We walked down a hallway and John stopped me in an empty corridor.

He asked, "How did you know how old the Life Magazine baby was?" "You told me, John!" I responded.

"People are coming to me asking why Dr. Bruner would pull the child's hand out and play around during such a dangerous procedure?" I said.

I was hoping John would relay this information to Dr. Bruner and he would change his story. In May 2000, an article published in the Atlanta Journal Constitution, by Maj McKenna, quoting Dr. Bruner:

"When Samuel's hand appeared in the uterine opening, I impulsively reached out and lifted it, it was a very human thing to do, to reach out and take someone's hand."

It worked! Bruner changed his story. I made copies of this article and posted them in the newsroom of the Tennessean. Nancy Rhoda said, "You still don't have vindication, Michael."

I passed Dolores Delvin in the hallway and she said, "Do you remember my friend you met at the surgery, the nurse, the one that introduced herself to you?" "Sure," I said. "She said they reach out all the time."

I decided to visit the Browns to get away.

John stood before his congregation and said, "God reached out and put his hand on this man's shoulder." He held up the Tennessean Newspaper that displayed the story, "The Picture That Went Around The World," I was an instant celebrity.

On another visit I met Fred Brown, no relation, and his wife Jeanne McDonald. Fred was a reporter with the Knoxville News Sentinel and he was writing a book about John's family. That same weekend I met two visitors from the Chattanooga area who were attending services at John's church that night. We talked about everything as we waited for time to leave. John told them about me being a newspaper photographer and not to hold that against me. Newspapers had not been kind to the serpent handling community.

Peggy mentioned there was a videotape of the snakebite that took their son's life. "You mean it was all caught on tape?" I asked. "Yeah, the sheriff's department confiscated the tape, and somehow the local television station got a hold of it. But when they played it on the news the bite was cut out. It's time to go," she said. I noticed, "Brother Glen," as John called him, put a cooler in the back of the minivan as the five of us piled in for the journey to John's church. Again, we sped along the winding road, "Jamie Coots will also be visiting tonight," he said.

Jamie Coots was the preacher at the True Tabernacle of Jesus Christ in Middlesboro, Kentucky, where Melinda was bitten in 1995.

"Jamie was hurt several weeks ago, a canebrake got him," John said.

"I've got ten rattlers in the cooler for Jamie," Brother Glen said.

Ten rattlers in the cooler! If John rolls this van on one of these curves and the cooler comes open, that would be two rattlers apiece. I white knuckled the armrest.

We passed a North Carolina State Trooper parked on the side of the road and John said,

"I've been pulled over many times and the trooper looked at the serpent box in the back seat and didn't say a word. They know what we're doing and they don't bother with us. There is supposed to be a television reporter at the service tonight," John said.

"We better hurry, there is no telling what them boys will do if he gets there before we do."

As we climbed the winding road to the church I could see the top of a live-remote television truck in the parking lot. "I can't believe he drove that truck up here!" I exclaimed.

We stood outside the church as Jamie Coots pulled into the parking lot. He reached into the back of his car and picked up a serpent box made of clear Plexiglas. It was awesome. Inside the box was a huge bright yellow canebrake rattlesnake. He greeted John with a hug. John introduced us and we shook hands. Jamie winced when I shook his hand and I realized that was the hand the rattler had bitten. His finger was deteriorating and I could see the bone. The reporter approached with his camera and John allowed him to film in the parking lot.

"Everyone is invited to worship the Lord but no cameras in the service," John said to him. This guy lowered his camera and shot the canebrake through the Plexiglas and then focused on Jamie's finger.

It was another incredible service. I watched as Jamie held the monster canebrake in his left hand. All of a sudden it struck at his right hand and Jamie pulled back before the rattler made contact. I felt like I was going to be sick. I needed to get up and get some air, but I dared not.

Jamie sat on the pew and struggled to remain conscious. The rest of the service was a blur; I couldn't wait for it to be over.

10 SERPENT HUNTING

During one of my trips to visit the Browns, John mentioned he was going to build an addition on his house, "just one room," he said. I offered to help. He accepted.

After the church service John, Mark, and Steve gathered around me. John said, "Mike, do you want to go hunting tomorrow?"

"What would we be hunting for in July?" I asked.

"Serpents," John replied.

"Absolutely," I responded. As I turned to walk away John said, "Bring your camera."

I rented a room at a local motel for the week. I didn't sleep much that night. The following morning we all met at John's house. I didn't have appropriate clothes for the occasion. What are appropriate clothes to wear serpent hunting anyway?

Steve had a place he was sure we would catch at least one. As we were driving, John pointed and said, "See that power line going up the mountain, Mike? That's where we're going."

We drove as far up the mountain as we could on an old logging road and parked. John, Mark, and Steve got snake hooks from the back of Steve's car. They were golf clubs with the head replaced by a hook. Steve also had a landing net like you would typically use fishing, but the net was replaced with heavy cloth. He led the way up the mountain.

I was absolutely terrified. I can't believe I'm doing this.

The sun was blistering. We hiked for a while and John said, "Now Mike, them boys get in a hurry and walk right past em. You be careful." Great! I thought.

Steve and Mark went ahead, and John and I walked together. After some time I heard Steve yell. John and I ran until we found him. They had one cornered under a big rock. I snapped pictures. Steve tried to poke his hook under the rock and drag the rattlesnake out. It didn't work. I leaned down and I could see it coiled up, ready to strike.

John Brown (left), Steve Frazier (center), Mark Brown (right)

The rattling sound was frightening. Mark went to the back of the rock and slid his hook under it. The rattlesnake came out with a fury. The three surrounded the snake and tried to pin it down. I was about fifteen feet away but that rattlesnake came right toward me. I turned to run and my feet slipped out from under me. My butt landed on solid rock. I bounced up and took off running. I thought John, Mark, and Steve were going to pee their pants they were laughing so hard. Finally, they were able to pin the snake down.

John lifted it with his hook and dropped it in the bag. The pillowcase was then twisted and thrown over the rim of the landing net. It was an ingenious way to transport a snake after capture.

I'd heard all the stories. Serpents taken up in church were pets. They were fed the night before, or milked of their venom so they wouldn't have any to inject. I also read that if a rattlesnake had eight rings on it's rattle then it's wild. If it has twenty it's been in captivity for some time. These were definitely wild!

John and I were talking as we tried to keep up with the others. I was exhausted, hot, and thirsty. John said, "We'll get a drink at a spring up ahead." I knew better but I was so thirsty. I followed John's lead and drank from the spring.

We all sat down to rest. Once again, they laughed so hard they cried at me trying to get away from that rattlesnake. Steve reached down and pulled his socks up and mentioned how comfortable his new snake boots were. I couldn't believe it. That is definitely the appropriate clothing to wear serpent hunting. I want some.

We took off once again and several minutes later I heard Mark yell. He found another one. This one seemed smaller than the first. This capture was much easier. Thank goodness! Now, as we walked the noise from the captured snakes was louder than ever. I'd had enough, but I tried not to show it. John said, "I could take up those serpents."

He knew I wanted to photograph him taking one up. What if he was bitten while I was taking pictures? We walked the last mile to the car. As we arrived John dumped the two rattlesnakes out on the ground. They used their hooks to control their movements but both were continuously striking at the air. I took pictures as John lifted one of the rattlesnakes with his hook.

He began speaking in tongues as he reached to stroke the back of the serpent with his bare hand. I was frozen. The moment I'd worked for and I could not take a picture. I was shaking as Steve and Mark were hypnotized watching John handle the rattlesnake.

He lowered the serpent to the ground and they put them in the box. I breathed a heavy sigh of relief.

Mark and I sat in the backseat on the drive home. We hit a bump and both serpents rattled. They were right behind me. I had my arm over the seat and I immediately pulled back. He noticed and put his arm across the back of the seat. On the next bump he made a hissing sound and pinched my shoulder, of course I jumped. He got a kick out of that.

We drove to a house and the basement contained approximately 20 aquariums. Each aquarium held a serpent. The room was hot and there was a terrible smell. As I walked by a tank a rattler struck at me but the glass enclosure stopped its strike. I tried to collect myself. Mark fed it a mouse so I could watch it strike and feed. That night I went back to my motel room and wrote everything down. I wanted to remember every detail about my serpent hunting experience.

The following Monday I returned to Nashville.

On assignment for the Tennessean I attended a benefit for the Vanderbilt Children's Hospital. The event was held at a home I call the Castle. It's a beautiful stone mansion across the street from the entrance to Percy Warner Park. My assignment was to photograph the speakers of the event. Their names were not on my assignment sheet. I arrived and introduced myself to my contact person. I took several pictures and the lady said it wouldn't be long now before the speakers arrived. I had another assignment fairly soon, I needed to leave.

"Oh, here they are now." She said. I turned and looked toward the door. Oh my goodness! Coming through the doorway was Dr. Bruner and Tulipan.

They went to the back of the home. I told my contact person, "Dr. Bruner will not want to see me. Let alone allow me take his photograph." I explained to her that I took the baby's hand picture and Dr. Bruner was furious with me. She went to talk to him and returned and said, "You're absolutely right, Dr. Bruner has locked himself in a back bedroom and is not coming out until you're off the property." I couldn't help but laugh at Dr. Bruner's antics.

I went back to the Tennessean and explained to Sam why I wasn't able to photograph the speakers of the event. He thought it was hilarious.

I worked when I could and about six weeks later returned to East Tennessee to visit the Browns. John had built the room addition on his house and I felt guilty I wasn't there to help. The inside was not finished. The next day I built a porch at the entrance to the addition while John was at work. The following day I did some minor sheetrock work on the inside and finished the pine wainscoting. John seemed pleased with my work.

That night he held a prayer service in the addition and six or eight people showed up. At one point in the service someone put their hand on my shoulder and it caught me off guard. I jumped. Then, everyone laid hands on me and some were speaking in tongues. It shouldn't have, but it scared me.

When I was building the porch I felt kind of sick. I had no endurance and the summer heat seemed to bother me more than usual.

It was more difficult than ever to return to freelancing for the Tennessean. I'd been using my trips to East Tennessee as an escape from the cloud of doubt surrounding my picture. After several months I received a fairly large check from Saba Press and all I could think of was getting away from everything. I decided I would take an apartment at what felt like a safe distance from the Browns' home. I moved to Morristown, Tennessee.

I was there two weeks when I started feeling really sick. I went to a local clinic and the doctor gave me a shot of highly concentrated penicillin. "That should knock out any infection you might have," he said.

Several weeks later I was still sick. The doctor said the initial infection had settled in my tonsils and I would have to have them removed. I remembered drinking from the creek the day we went serpent hunting. I wondered if that's what made me sick. The following week I had my tonsils removed.

When I woke up after the surgery, Peggy Brown was sitting beside my hospital bed. I was never happier to see anyone in my life.

"I knowed you were by yourself and I just couldn't not come," Peggy said. "Thank you, I hoped my Dad would come but he didn't," I said. She stayed for a while and said she had to get home before John got off work.

After a little while a nurse came, helped me to a wheelchair and called a cab for me. I had no other way to get home. I remember the doctor saying eat all the ice cream you want. The cab dropped me off and I settled in on my couch. I began to wonder if I was going to live through this. The swelling in my throat would not go down. I'd been on my couch a week and I could barely drink water let alone eat ice cream. I was weak; I was starving. I've never felt so alone.

I called my little brother in Nashville and I was crying. I explained how sick I was. He said, "Just get yourself here and I'll take care of you." Somehow I packed a bag and drove the three hours to David's house. He did exactly what he said he would; he took great care of me.

I stayed a week on his couch and felt good enough to go home. I recovered from the surgery but a severe depression set in. A gentleman named Jim Agresti called and wanted an interview about the baby's hand picture. We began a dialogue. I talked him through the story. He titled his article, "Struggling Photographer Chooses Principle Over Money." He posted the story on his web site, www.justfacts.com.

I've never felt suicidal in my life but I was starting to wonder how I was going to get out of this terrible depression. I found myself completely overcome. I didn't leave the condo, ever. I could not face the world. "God, please help me."

My friend Eddie called; he could tell something was very wrong. We'd been friends for 12 years. He said, "Pack everything in a U-haul and come to Wisconsin." I didn't know what else to do. I felt like he was throwing me a lifeline. I did exactly that. They were very nice and had a room all set up for me. I put my furniture in storage and took a week to rest.

I was really feeling better and more determined than ever to tell the story behind my picture. I faxed my story to News Photographer Magazine, Photo District News, and I also sent a copy to Frank Sutherland, Executive News Editor of the Tennessean Newspaper. He assigned a reporter and the guy called me. I was hopeful but he turned out to be some flunky that had no idea what he was doing. It went absolutely nowhere.

I stayed with Eddie and his family several months and decided to return to Nashville. A lady from Pennsylvania Right to Life called, she wanted to put my picture on eight billboards. She had talked to Marcel and he told her it would cost $2,000 apiece. I called Marcel the next day and he said I could give her use of the picture if I wanted to, but I would owe him his fifty percent. Was I prepared to send him $8,000, of course not. This made me very uncomfortable. Would I ever get my negatives back if I fired him?

I could tell by the monthly statements from Saba Press demand for the picture tapered off in January 2001. I received several calls that stated the people at Saba Press were very rude when they found out they were pro-life. I called Marcel and said, "I appreciate everything you've done but I want to represent the picture myself."

11 THE BATTLE BEGINS

I was not going to allow this picture to fade into obscurity. It's a Miracle! I intended to create a web site, post the picture and tell my story. Surely some gung-ho reporter would be curious and research the facts. Several weeks later I received a phone call from a UPS driver. He was trying to make a delivery to an old address. Thank goodness he had the correct phone number. The next day the package arrived and sure enough it was the negatives from Saba.

I wanted www.michaelclancy.com as the URL for my web site, but a Michael Clancy in California already owned it. I found him through the "Who Is Registry" and told him my story. He was an insurance salesman and intended to use the site for business. He agreed to sell it to me for what he had in it, $75. Within two months I had a simple web site up and running.

I stayed up four days emailing every pregnancy center I could find an email address for. I stated the picture would always be available on my site to counsel an unplanned pregnancy. I was amazed at the response. I didn't count on being attacked. Yes, I had prints for sale but to be called a pro-life profiteer was something I didn't anticipate. I did receive positive email but the negative ones kept me up at night.

I searched the web for people and organizations I thought would want to help me. I emailed The Alliance Defense Fund and told them my story. I did get an immediate response. The email said I would never be able to prove the unborn child reached out on its own. I emailed Americans United for Life, The Thomas Moore Center for Law & Justice and I received responses from both groups, but no help.

Again, another all-nighter led me to send an email to the web site of Norma McCorvey, the Roe, of Roe v Wade. She is now Catholic and affiliated with Father Frank Pavone of Priests for Life. He contacted me in response and asked if I would be willing to be on his television show, "Defending Life." It would be taped and shown at a later date around the world. "Sure," I said.

July 10, 2002, I flew to Birmingham, Alabama and did the taping at The Eternal Word Television Network studio. I met Fr. Frank Pavone and Joe Scheidler. He was also a guest on the show.

Making people aware of your presence on the web is not easy. In it's first six months online my web site only received several hundred visitors.

I was listening to the G. Gordon Liddy Show one day and he was talking about abortion. I went home that night and emailed his show. One of his producers, Diana, called me the following morning and asked if I would do an interview with Mr. Liddy. I was very excited and said, "Yes!"

On August 13, 2002, Diana called and I did the interview. Mr. Liddy was very gracious. That week my web site received 10,000 visitors. Rush Limbaugh talked about my picture on his radio show and Mr. Liddy's site displayed a link to mine. People started emailing and mentioned how they learned of my story.

Two days after the G. Gordon Liddy interview I received an email from Dr. Ray Paschall. He was the Director of Anesthesia for the Vanderbilt University Fetal Surgery Program. The following email was dated 15 August 2002, 11:51 a.m.:

Dear Michael,

I trust you have better journalistic integrity than is demonstrated by your commentary with the fetal picture at your web site. I am the Vanderbilt anesthesiologist involved with all fetal surgeries and your description of events is entirely inaccurate and reads like a fairy tale rather than a scientific accomplishment. The fetus has never moved an arm purposely or exhibited muscle strength because it is anesthetized, two babies have exhibited withdrawal to surgical stimulus which made us modify our technique by increasing fetal analgesia. Because of the delicate nature of the surgery, it could not be performed on a fetus capable of moving. We always anesthetize the fetus to make an appropriate surgical field for Dr. Tullipan and he gives me feedback on the operating conditions. I am offended by your misrepresentation because most of the public would not know better and you are deceiving them and causing ethical consternations beyond the dramatic picture you are trying to sell for personal gain.

I do not know how much dramatic licensure you are granting yourself, but the story is unbelievable for those of us who are there each and every time. Remember that you are just following in the footsteps of two other photographers in taking this staged picture, give credit to Ann Rayner and Max Aguillera for getting the fetal hand shot first.

The photo cannot be carried out without Dr. Bruner reaching in and grasping the hand, the baby does not move and the uterus does not shake. That has never happened and never will happen because it is physically impossible.

I have seen these pictures many times over and the suggestion that you have captured something unique is deceptive and now seems to be a money grabbing scheme given the verbage associated with your web site. Why?

I will refute any attempt to portrary your description as accurate and will get Dr. Bruner and Dr. Tullipan to do the same. We are happy to have our work chronicled but prefer it to be described accurately and professionally without fluff.

Ray Paschall M.D.

My response was as follows, dated 15 August, 2002, 1:51 p.m.:

Dear Dr. Paschall,

Thank you so much for your wonderful email.

For the sake of brevity, I will not answer the charges you have stated against me.

I do however, appreciate your attempt at explaining the process involved to attain, "good anesthesia". The sacrifices that you have made to become a leader in your field are also noted, and admired.

The next time you have a chance to sit down and talk, one on one, to John Howser, ask him if the picture that Max Aguilerra Helweg shot, was meant to be on the cover of Life Magazines December, 1999 issue. (Their Millennium Issue, to show how far medical science had progressed in the twentieth century, inutero fetal surgery) John is a wonderfully honest man and a redness will appear on his face. Note his uneasiness at answering the question, for he won't be able to lie without this being detected.

It was John Howser that leaked to me the information that I had scooped the Millennium cover of Life Magazine. In turn, I had a picture agency call Life Magazine and offer my picture to them. On the initial phone call, I stated, I have a picture that scoops your planned, December cover. They were livid.

Mr. Helweg posed his photograph in July 1999. The picture I have was taken August 1999. After which I went into an intensive negotiation with Life Magazine. Life Magazine wanted to purchase all rights to my photograph, and this is a quote, "to kill it." They wanted to stop my picture from ever being published. This is documented.

During the negotiations with Life magazine, I told them that the hospital had leaked the fact that the child in Mr. Helweg's picture was twenty-four weeks in utero. That they had to put my picture on the cover of the December 1999 issue because it was real, and "my baby" was twenty-one weeks, the youngest they will ever operate on. I then told Life Magazine, during the negotiations, that if they didn't use my picture, I would find a picture agency to aggressively market my picture and the story would be old news by the time the December issue of Life Magazine was published. That is exactly what happened. Life Magazine buried the story, "Born Twice", in the last pages of the December issue.

It was also reported to me that when Anne Raynor came back from vacation, and found out what had happened. That some freelance photographer "grabbed" a miracle photograph, and scooped the proposed cover of Life Magazine, she was furious. She then proceeded to pose incredible photographs, very similar to mine, and distribute them to whoever called looking for the 'famous' photograph, (my photograph).

So, you see, I am absolutely positive that you were not at Vanderbilt in the capacity you now enjoy, in August 1999. Or is it your contention that Dr. Joseph P. Bruner posed the picture that cost him the cover of Life Magazines' Millennium Issue? That... is the whole truth.

I do agree that my beginners' attempt at a website does appear to be a money grab and I will be making changes to reflect the mission that is now very clear to me.

Very Sincerely, Michael Clancy

There were two more emails from Dr. Paschall that followed, with my response to each.

Dated 17 August 2002, 7:18 a.m.:

Hello Michael,

I have run fetal surgery since 1997. Fact and end of that discussion. The point is not relevant, the claim that a baby reached up is the erroneous point. I have missed maybe 5 surgeries for various reasons out of all our series. I would have still been the director and my pathway would have been followed. I will not identfy the patients, but 2 babies showed withdrawal movements from surgical stimulatiop, at which point we administer more relaxant and analgesia.

I will trust you on when Max and Ann did whatever and in what time frame, I am only bothered by the factually erroneous claim that the baby "reached" up and grabbed Joe. Our team would have met and discussed the implications of that event. I have been here and directed fetal in utero anesthesia since 1997, so if your picuture is 1999 I was here and directing the case. That is an indesputable fact.

Please get the story factually correct without dramatic enhancement and I am happy to give you and pictorial credit you wish. I don't care about any of those workings. Since we have passed NIH review and its questions on fetal ethics and have been named the only center to perform this procedure in the U.S., I want the reports to be factually correct. The fetus in your picture did NOT reach up and grab Dr. Bruner and whatever anonymous nurse commented on that purported event was most likely the least experienced person in the room.

Correct your "story" attachment by making the point clear that your photo is a staged shot and then you will have presented a close enough to factually accurate presentation to satisfy our problem with your claim. The moment captured would still be moving, however please do not make false storyline dramaticzation to sell the picture.

Ray Paschall M.D.

My response, dated 17 August 2002, 4:52 p.m.:

Dear Dr. Paschall,

I have the living proof on film. When I clicked the shutter of my camera and held my motor drive on continuous, I documented in four frames, Samuel responding to Dr. Bruners touch. I know what I saw.

With all due respect, we will just have to agree, to disagree.

Thank you for your email.

Michael Clancy

Third email from Dr. Paschall dated 17 August 2002, 1:48 p.m.:

No Michael,

You do not know what you saw and I wil go forward with Dr.Bruner thru Vanderbilt legal channels if you do not change the story which is entirely inaccurate. Factually that did not occur and I will not agree to disagree. Ask Dr. Bruner. I had been in on at least 2 shots that were staged prior to your photodocumentation. It did not happen as you seem to think and must be corrected. Ask Dr. Bruner to respond and he will give you the facts. I am now convinced you were deceived because our team knew the event and I am sure presumed you would also.

I will not agree to disagree, because this is a factual dispute with objective evidence not subjective.

This is a bigger matter than you perceive, drop the exaggeration or hire a lawyer because it is an absolute inaccuracy as written. The picture is great, the story is not.

Ray Paschall M.D.

After receiving the emails from Dr. Paschall threatening legal action against me if I didn't change my web site to reflect his demands my fear escalated.

Every now and then someone would email me and say, "There is no telling how many babies lives your picture has saved." I became so emotional I would cry for days after one of these emails. "Why God, have you chosen me?

I'm reminded of the verse, "To whomsoever much is given, of him much will be required," Luke 12:48. Not only did I feel this tremendous responsibility to share the picture with the world, I had to correct the misinformation that was out there. There were sites that displayed the Life Magazine picture of Sarah Marie claiming it was Samuel. Others stated Samuel was 24 weeks at the time of the surgery.

I searched the web over and over again for Samuel Armas, Dr. Joseph Bruner, and even my name. I emailed web site after web site and offered a beautiful copy of the picture if they would correct their errors.

Life Magazine posted Sarah's picture on one of their web sites and claimed it caused the end of Matt Drudge's television career.

I announced on my web site I would donate the picture to pro-life groups and pregnancy centers. People misunderstood and emailed me for their free 8x10 print. I sent out hundreds, free, and began to get bombarded with email.

Some were thanking me for the picture and others wanted to know if I was going to pay for the college education of all the unwanted children after abortion became illegal.

One gentleman just found out his wife was pregnant with twins. He was in a panic because the doctor said they have spina bifida. He wanted the contact information for the fetal surgery team so they could get the same surgery Samuel had. I felt terrible for him because I knew twins would never be considered for the surgery.

Another gentleman and his wife were sent to a counselor after learning of her pregnancy. The counselor told them they were going to have a spina bifida baby and he recommended an abortion. He said, "We're Christian and have always been active in the pro-life community, but, behind closed doors we questioned our faith, we questioned our strength. Could we truly raise a child we had to do everything for it's entire life?"

On the day little Emilia was born he was looking over the nurses' shoulder as she got her first medical exam. He was so excited he said, "She's supposed to have spina bifida." The nurse turned the little girl over and said, "See the birthmark on her back, that gives a false positive to the spina bifida test. He went on to say he broke down thinking just how close he came to aborting his baby girl.

Another email was from a woman that could not get the voices of the five babies she aborted out of her head.

A Catholic priest felt compelled to email me and tell me about the night my picture reminded him of. He was volunteering at a local hospital. In the middle of the night he was called to be with twin brother and sister, born at nineteen weeks. He gave last rights and held their hands until he felt the life leave their tiny bodies.

An email from a nurse told how she carries the babies, born too premature to try to save, in her scrubs pocket. She felt they should feel the warmth of another human being and not be left alone on a counter to die.

Then there's the emails from men that paid to abort the only child they would have had and not a day goes by they don't think about that baby.

Another email from a grandmother thanked me for the life of her only grandchild because her daughter saw the picture and couldn't go through with her planned abortion.

Why me Lord? What can I do to help these people?

Whenever I think I can't keep telling this story I remember the email I have on the wall of my office. It sustains me.

"Dear Michael, There are countless children out there who will never meet or hear of you who owe their very lives to you."

12 WANDERER

I put together a fresh portfolio together and began to search for a full time job as a newspaper photographer. I interviewed at the Pantagraph in Bloomington, Illinois. The Tribune-Eagle in Cheyenne, Wyoming, and the Rockford Register Star in Rockford, Illinois. I was blessed to receive an offer from the Rockford Register Star. Brad Burt was the photo editor. He said, "I received close to 100 portfolios and yours was the best, by far."

The second anniversary of 9-11 came and I was in a hotel room searching the Yellow Pages for an apartment. After working there close to seven months, I returned from shooting my assignments for the day. Brad said, "A lady from Newsweek called and wants you to call her back." They wanted to publish the baby's hand picture in their June

2003 issue. A photographer has already been sent to photograph Samuel for the article.

He is now 3 1/2 years old. Wow, I was finally going to get my picture published in Newsweek. When that issue hit the newsstands I went to three different bookstores and bought every copy I could find. I'd waited a very long time for this.

July 7, 2003 I received an email from Robert Wasinger, Senior Policy Advisor with Senator Sam Brownback's office in Washington, DC. He requested I testify before a Senate Subcommittee Hearing regarding my experience taking the picture. Samuel's parents were going to offer testimony about the surgical procedure on their unborn baby. I was also invited to be present at the White House as President Bush signs the Partial Birth Abortion Ban into law.

Everyone was hoping the Senate Hearing and the signing ceremony would take place within the same week. That didn't happen.

On September 25, 2003 I entered the Hart Senate Building in Washington, D.C. and found my way to Senator Brownback's office. I met Rob Wasinger and Dr. James Thorpe. Dr. Thorpe is a specialist in Maternal Fetal Medicine and would be offering testimony. He knew of my picture and was stunned to learn Dr. Bruner was claiming Samuel was under anesthesia and could not have reached out on his own.

When the time came for us to go to the hearing we left the room and walked down the hallway. Alex and Julie Armas had been waiting in another room with Samuel. Rob opened a door and I saw them for the first time since our meeting at the Atlanta hospital when Samuel was born. It was incredibly exciting for me to watch Samuel run down the hallway in front of us. He had light leg braces that hindered his movement but didn't slow him down.

I sat in the back of the hearing room to gather my thoughts and Dr. Thorpe noticed my uneasiness. He reassured me I would do a great job. The room started filling up with people. An aide came up to me and said, "This is highly unusual to see so many people at a Commerce Committee Hearing." With a big smile on his face he said, "They must be here to see Samuel."

We all gave our testimony and it was unforgettable. After the hearing Senator Brownback asked me to walk with him to his bus. We talked and as we approached the bus he introduced me to Senator Rick Santorum. We said our goodbyes and they got on the bus.

I returned to my job in Rockford. One day as I was cleaning house my phone rang. I looked at the caller ID and there were no numbers, it said, "The White

House." My hand was shaking as I answered. I was invited to attend the signing of the Ban on Partial Birth Abortion into law on November 5, 2003. It was originally intended to be at the White House but the number of attendees grew so large it had been moved to the Ronald Reagan Building and International Trade Center.

It was an emotional event for me. I was told they planned to have Samuel on stage with President Bush as he signed the bill. But, Julie Armas was pregnant and her doctor wouldn't allow her to fly. I stood outside afterwards not wanting the momentous occasion to be over. I noticed a gentleman with several men standing around him. After a closer look I realized the man was Dr. James Dobson. I marched right over to him, stuck out my hand, and said, "Dr. Dobson, I just want to thank you for giving my picture such great publicity in your Focus On The Family Ministry." I explained I took the picture of Samuel reaching from the womb. He was so excited to meet me he exclaimed to several others, "He took that picture!" We shook hands. I couldn't believe it, I just met Dr. James Dobson and he was excited to meet me!

I tried to distance myself from the suspicion and doubt by taking the job in Rockford. Now, all I could think about was going home to Nashville and renewing my campaign to tell my story.

I must talk to the Switzer family. Trish Switzer was the subject of the Life Magazine article and I know the editors at "Life" must have told them their picture was planned to be on the cover. I started searching for Mike and Trish Switzer. The Life Magazine article stated he was an Army Major and they lived in Maryland but that was six years ago.

I quit the job at the Rockford Register Star and returned to Nashville in early 2005. I again started freelancing for the Tennessean.

A huge break came when TV Guide called and asked if I could shoot the annual Country Music Festival for them. It was June 9-12, 2005, in downtown Nashville. There were many country music stars scheduled to perform. To cover an event like this with TV Guide credentials dangling around my neck was unbelievable.

The stars managers recognized I was shooting for TV Guide and photo opportunities just presented themselves. Everybody wanted to be in TV Guide. Trace Adkins, Steve Azar, Dierks Bentley, Big & Rich, Brad Cotter, Cowboy Troy, Billy Currington, Josh Gracin, Jo Dee Messina, Montgomery Gentry, Jon Randall, Rascal Flatts, LeAnn Rimes, Julie Roberts, Trick Pony, Keith Urban, Phil Vassar, Jimmy Wayne, Mark Wills, Gretchen Wilson, Darryl Worley, Carrie Underwood, Dolly Parton and

Michelle Wright were just some of the stars in attendance. It was a lot of fun!

While I was in Rockford technology advanced to a level that if you wanted to be a freelance photographer you had to have the ability to transmit pictures from the event. Which meant I had to have a laptop computer and cell phone to transmit images.

When I didn't have assignments I picked up work as a handyman drawing from my experience as a carpenter. One day, Bill Steber and I were working in the photo department and he said, "I haven't had a shower in months." "You don't smell that bad Bill," I said. He laughed and told me they had a leak in their bathroom. The plumber left them with a cut off copper pipe sticking straight out of the wall.

"I have to sit in the tub and the water hits my chest," Bill said. I offered to go to their house and see if I could fix their plumbing problems. I ended up redoing their entire bathroom.

Pat Casey and Bill were married. Both were staff photographers at the Tennessean. They had a very old house that needed a lot of work. Which turned out to be very lucky for me.

I mentioned to Pat one day I desperately needed the capability to transmit pictures. She said, "I'll buy the laptop for you and you just work it off. There's plenty for you to do around here." My immediate reaction was, "Oh no Pat, I couldn't do that." She said, "I want to."

I was living in a terrible little apartment in East Nashville. The drive to Pat's house was 40 minutes each way. It was quite a hike on a daily basis.

In a 24-hour period, three people were murdered within a mile of my apartment. So, I started looking for a place to live closer to Murfreesboro. I was blessed to stumble on a little farmhouse for $450 a month. I talked to the landlord at my apartment and he let me out of my lease for an extra month's rent.

The farm had eight acres and three horses were boarded in the field next to the house. This little farmhouse had so much character I fell in love with it, and the horses. I called them my roommates and carrots became a permanent item on my grocery list.

My new landlord told me a little old lady lived there for fifty years. She sat in the swing on the front porch all day on Sundays and read her Bible. Miss Nora passed away and the house had been empty for two years. I'd been reading my Bible regularly. Now, I read out loud to the ghost of Miss Nora Barrett. It might sound crazy. By now, I probably was.

I counted my blessings every day. I knew God brought me this good fortune.

I received an email requesting I share my story at a pro-life event in Hendersonville, Tennessee. I'd been asked many times before but this time was different. I said I would do it. I was a nervous wreck but everything turned out well.

My next event came in a round about way and I shared my story at a banquet to benefit a pregnancy center in Murfreesboro. Vicky Edwards was the director. I was incredibly shy and it took everything I had in me to take the stage in front of all those people. I spoke for ten minutes and when I turned to walk away from the podium people jumped out of their chairs to clap for me. I couldn't believe it. Ms. Edwards came up afterwards and said, "Michael, I have done this for twenty years. That was the first standing ovation I've ever gotten for a speaker and last year we had Oliver North."

People lined up to speak to me and blessed me with encouraging words. Many said, "You have got to continue sharing your story." My faith grew stronger than ever after the banquet.

I contacted a local television reporter, Dennis Ferrier, and told him my story. He brought a crew to the farm and interviewed me for three hours. I had no idea when the piece would air. I got lucky one night channel checking the news broadcasts, and there I was. As fast as I could I popped in a VHS tape and recorded what was left of the interview. Dennis won 1st place from the Associated Press, best hard news story of the year, 2006, for the state of

Tennessee. The piece was titled, "Miracle." He claimed the five-minute interview was the longest of the year. They mentioned nothing about Life Magazine but interviewed John Howser at Vanderbilt. When asked how the picture came to be John said, "Someone asked how big is the baby and the doctor pulled the hand out to show how big it was." That was an absolute lie.

As time passed I grew more and more frustrated the newspaper wouldn't do a follow up article regarding the picture. One day I worked myself up and knocked on the door of the new managing editor. Her name was Meg Downey and she motioned me in. She looked over both articles and said, "I believe we gave both sides an opportunity to tell their story." She didn't support another article.

That afternoon in the photo department Tom Stanford approached me and said, "Michael, I can't begin to tell you how big a mistake it was to just walk into the managing editors' office. It takes me a week to see her and I run the department." "It was something I had to do," I said. His response, "You did this to yourself, you have no one else to blame." The Tennessean quit using me after that. I was now working at Pat and Bill's to survive.

I've always believed if you want something bad enough picture it done. Not only picture it done, but live as if it's already happened. I contacted

Ambassador Speaker's Bureau and asked them if they would be interested in representing me. I met with Gloria Leyda and Wes Yoder, the owner. I signed an exclusive three-year contract and they immediately started booking events for me. I was terrified at the prospect of public speaking, but I knew I had to exhaust every avenue to expose the truth. The first few events were absolutely traumatic for me. Overcoming my shyness was impossible. I worked on my speech and put a few pictures on a flash drive for my presentation. The audiovisual equipment at each event began to play an important role. The first few events I could barely see the picture on the screen because the projector was bad. After all, it's all about the picture.

13 THE COMMUNITY OF FAITH CHURCH

I received an email from the Pastor of The Community Of Faith Church in Carterville, Illinois, Todd Greiner. He wanted to use the picture in a full-page ad in their local newspaper, the Southern Illinoisian. I sent him a file of the picture and their ad published April 11, 2007. Pastor Todd sent me a copy and it looked fantastic.

The morning of May 4, 2007, I was awakened by the familiar ping of newly arrived email. There were several emails telling me the TV show "House" recreated my picture in an episode called, "Fetal Position." It aired the night before and it was very exciting to receive the email from those that saw it. Wow, things are happening. God is at work.

Pastor Todd emailed again on June 22, 2007. This time he and his congregation wanted to publish the same full page ad in USA Today. The cost for them would be, his word, "astronomical." Over the next several months, he worked with the ad department at USA Today. They claimed the picture was too graphic. This was unbelievable considering I shot the picture for them and they published it in full color for their story about spina bifida.

The picture was changed to black and white and still it was too graphic. Pastor Todd joked with me, "Maybe I could get more publicity if I called Sean Hannity and told him that USA Today refused to run our ad." He made several more submissions and the final image was almost unrecognizable from the original picture. The ad published on August 6, 2007, on page 5 of the A section, for a fee of $75,000.

Jeff Johnson with American Family Radio Network contacted me and asked if I would do an interview August 7, 2007. It lasted for 25 minutes.

Pastor Todd called and said, "Michael, you need a few days of R & R. Would you consider driving up for a visit next weekend and sharing your story with our congregation? Sue and I have a few acres with a pond and it's very private." "Absolutely", I said.

I realized as I drove I would be stepping up to the podium on August 19, 2007, the eighth anniversary of taking the picture. The drive was a little over three hours.

Pastor Todd asked me if I would take a walk with him. "It's gorgeous here Todd, you are blessed," I said.

"God gave me something to say to you Michael. Do not let man steal your joy." Tears welled up in my eyes because that is exactly what I'd done. I allowed the doctor's denial of the picture to take away my joy.

We had a very relaxing weekend and I shared my story with his congregation on Sunday morning. After the service Pastor Todd and I went into his office and he handed me an envelope. "Should I open it?" I asked. "Yes," he replied. It was a check for $9,500! "Todd, I can't accept this," I said. "You don't have a choice," he replied. "Our congregation took up a collection for you." I couldn't help it, I cried uncontrollably.

Pastor Todd, Sue and I met several members of his church at a restaurant for lunch. Afterward, we said our goodbyes.

I cried most of the way home and thanked God for blessing me.

I prayed about what to do with the money. I ordered a small extremely powerful projector I could take to events and created a presentation in Keynote. I had a VHS tape of Samuel and I testifying before the Senate Hearing. I converted it to digital and included several clips in my new presentation. I also bought a remote control to advance my slides. Now I would be able to deliver a very powerful visual presentation with my speech. I shared my story at ten events the last three months of 2007.

On September 22, 2007 I spoke at the 34th Annual Right to Life of Michigan Affiliate Conference in Lansing. A gentleman, Dr. Daniel J. Pepin, came up to me immediately after I left the podium and said, "Don't ever get good at telling that story." I was crushed. Then I realized what he meant. I was not a polished speaker and that's what made my story have such an impact. Each event left me emotionally and physically drained.

14 OLD FRIENDS

An old friend saw the Dennis Ferrier interview on television and emailed me. Don Anderson had been the circulation manager at The Review Appeal in Franklin, Tennessee when I worked there. I hadn't seen him in 12 years. He was retired and living thirty minutes away in Spring Hill, Tennessee.

We made plans to get together. I don't know whether he was more interested in seeing the horses, or me, but he was really excited to be coming for a visit.

After he arrived we walked around the farm and I asked him, "Have you kept in touch with anyone from the old days?" "Do you remember Juanita?" he replied. "Of course I remember Juanita. I had a crush on her. But she was married with three kids. What's she been up to?" I asked. "She's divorced and lives in Amelia Island, Florida. She has a great job and her kids are all grown," he said.

Don took out his cell phone and dialed a number. He said, "Hello, Juanita?" and started talking to her. He then handed me the phone. "No Don, don't do that to me," I said. He kept holding the phone out and I finally took it from him. "Hello," I said, "Juanita, what have you been up to?" We talked for a few minutes and I handed the phone back. That was the beginning.

Juanita and I followed up by exchanging email. Don told her about my picture. "I'm so proud of you," she said. I didn't realize how powerful those words could be. It had been a long time since I'd heard them.

We started exchanging email on a regular basis. We graduated to phone calls and pretty soon were talking daily. I bought a headset, like mine, and sent it to her. It's great; you can wash dishes and talk on the phone.

I suggested we read out loud to each other from our Bibles. I would read a chapter and she would read a chapter. I explained in theory, if we could read ten pages a day we could read the entire 1,200-page Bible in four months. It was a plan I was trying to stick to on my own.

There were constantly things happening that reminded me of just how big God is.

July 3 2008, I was a featured speaker at the National Right To Life Convention, at the Crystal City Hyatt Regency in Arlington, Virginia. Also featured were Senator Fred Thompson, Karl Rove, and Fr. Richard Newhouse. I was blessed to meet many of the people I'd corresponded with over the years because of the picture.

Juanita came to visit twice. During her first visit I took her to Centerville, Tennessee to the church she attended when she lived there. They were having their Homecoming and she was very excited to be going. So excited in fact that when we stopped at a little market for a soda she came out and got in the white Explorer next to mine. She apologized to the driver and they shared a laugh.

The church reunion was fun and Juanita reminisced as we drove through her old stomping grounds. We went to the Narrows of the Harpeth River afterwards and hiked to the top of the ridge.

The day before she was supposed to fly home I asked her to stay a few more days and she seemed excited. "Sure," she said. I called Southwest Airlines and changed her flight home.

She spent some time looking for a job and said she wanted to move back to Tennessee. The extra days passed quickly and I was really sad to see her leave.

Things returned to normal and our phone calls resumed. One night we talked so late I literally fell asleep on the phone. She stills laughs about that.

Two months later, she came back and this time she was determined to find a job. She did, at Preferred Property Management right here in Murfreesboro. She would be doing the same thing she was doing at her current job.

The Bible says if you are single stay that way because being married takes you away from Christ. I'd been single for almost twenty years and I just didn't want to be alone any longer. I prayed that if it was His will for me, "Please send me a good woman." I prayed this prayer many times before my old friend Don Anderson found me again.

Juanita and I married on October 2, 2008, under the massive tree in the front yard of the little farmhouse. It was just the three of us, our preacher, Pastor Phillip Robinson from New Vision Baptist Church, and Juanita and I. It was blessed. She brought love into my life. That changed everything.

15 COLONEL MIKE SWITZER

Back in 2005, I had an assignment at the Army National Guard Base on Sidco Drive. I met an Army Public Relations Officer and asked him if I were looking for someone in the Army how could I go about locating them? He gave me his card and told me to call him. He was Randy D. Harris, Director of Public Affairs-Houston Barracks. A week later I sent him an email requesting he forward my contact information to Major Mike Switzer.

Weeks passed by and I couldn't believe it, Mike Switzer received the information and emailed me. He was in England training pilots but was eventually being transferred to Huntsville, Alabama where he planned to retire from the Army. He'd been promoted to Colonel. What luck, Huntsville is a two-hour drive from my house. I said I'd love to interview him about the Life Magazine article if he would allow me, but would wait until he moved to Huntsville.

Juanita knew most of my story and just how important meeting with Colonel Switzer might be. She pushed me; it was actually more of a gentle nudge to set up the meeting during her second visit. Three years had passed since I corresponded with him through email. Surely he was settled in Huntsville by now? Maybe retired? I sent an email to him and he responded.

On Sunday morning, August 24, 2008 we drove the 110 miles to meet him at a Ruby Tuesday's restaurant off Interstate 565, just outside Huntsville. He wasn't at all what I expected.

I wanted to hear he and Trish were told the picture Max Hellweg shot of their daughter, Sarah Marie, was going to be on the cover. He said they didn't know about that until later.

Dr. Bruner asked the Switzers if they would participate with the Life Magazine Story. Their only contact with the magazine was with the reporter, Skip Hollandsworth, and photographer, Max Aguilera-Hellweg.

They had dinner with Max and Skip and talked about the story they were doing. The Switzer's were told that after they signed the consent forms they would have basically no rights regarding the article.

The Switzers were happy to be included to draw attention to the medical condition, spina bifida.

16 EVENT-MANIA

I've been blessed to share my story at over 110 events in three countries. I've met the most incredible people. Heroes. That's the word that comes to mind.

A most unforgettable event for me was a benefit for the Come Alive Ministry in Winder, Georgia, just outside Atlanta. I was told days before the event Julie Armas would be a guest speaker and everyone was hoping she would bring Samuel.

Wow! I haven't seen Samuel since the Senate Hearing in 2003. I was sitting at the front table when Julie and Samuel arrived. He sat in a chair directly opposite me. Julie sat to his left and said, "Samuel, do you know who this man is?" and pointed to me. He looked at me and shook his head, no. "He's the man that took the picture." Samuel looked at me and a huge smile came over his face.

Julie spoke first and showed a slideshow of Samuel growing up. It was fantastic and I couldn't help but tear up. As she ended her talk she asked for Samuel to come to the podium. He stood and walked to the steps at the front of the stage, but the braces on his legs would not allow him to bend them enough to climb the steps and for a fraction of a second, he stood still. His father immediately came and whisked him up the steps to his mother's side. He was seven years old now and as he stood next to Julie he slid his arm around her leg and turned to face the crowd. The audience erupted in a thunderous applause.

It was a magical night as I stood at the podium and shared my story. A single floodlight shined on me, spilling light on a chair in front of the stage. Samuel sat in that illuminated chair and his was the only face I could see during my entire presentation. The rest of the room was in silhouette. He was turned completely around, resting his chin on the back of his chair. Smiling.

I spoke at another event for a pregnancy center just outside Dallas. Twenty or so people lined up to talk to me afterwards. A woman kept moving to the back of the line. It was obvious she wanted to be the last person to speak to me. She and I, and a gentleman sitting off to the side were the only ones left. He must be waiting for her I thought. "I saw your baby's hand picture in a newspaper ad for this event." She said, as she took my hands in hers. "I knew I had to come here, meet you and tell you about the first time I saw it. I can't even remember the publication but I felt like I'd been punched in the stomach. How could I ever have convinced myself it wasn't a baby? I cried for days not being able to go to work and I will be forever changed by that picture," she said.

At another event a young woman desperately wanted to tell me something but couldn't stop crying uncontrollably long enough to speak. I wish I had done whatever it took to know the source of her pain.

January 24, 2009 I attended an event at Faneuil Hall in Boston for the Massachusetts Citizens For Life. The event had been planned for seven months. It's a very historic place. Samuel Adams delivered speeches encouraging independence from Great Britain there.

On November 7, 1979 Faneuil Hall was the site of Senator Edward M. Kennedy's speech declaring his candidacy for president. On November 3, 2004 it was the site of Senator John Kerry's concession speech for the presidential election.

I walked on that very stage as the keynote speaker five days after the special election to fill Senator Ted Kennedy's seat. The members of the Massachusetts Citizens For Life made 178,000 phone calls to help elect Scott Brown to fill the vacated Senate seat. Brown became the 41st vote, breaking the Democrats control of the 60 votes needed in the Senate to overcome filibusters.

This changed everything and I thanked the attendees that afternoon for giving the rest of us hope. They were proof you can make a difference.

I shared my story at an event in Hartford, Connecticut April 29, 2010 for the ABC Women's Center. After my presentation a woman came up to me as I greeted people and said, "You must come to Nigeria." "I don't think so," I said, and smiled at her. "No, Michael you must come to Nigeria." I gave her my business card and told her to call me.

I called Juanita after the event and told her I had a request to go to Nigeria. "I'm not going to Nigeria," I said. "Michael, if that's what God wants you have no choice but to go," she said. She is my rock. Of course I must go.

The woman did call several days later. Her name was Olabisi (Bisi) Chukwudile. Again she said, "Michael, you must come to Nigeria. I am the founder of Lifechoice International and I want to sponsor your trip. I told her I would do as many events as she could arrange in a one-week period. That week turned into two and Bisi set up three events in Lagos, and two more in Abuja, the capitol of Nigeria.

I boarded a twelve-hour non-stop flight from Atlanta to Lagos, Nigeria on September 3, 2010.

The Lagos Airport was extremely drab and there were military soldiers carrying machine guns everywhere. They had 40 round banana clips and it was very intimidating.

I was extremely tired as I approached the luggage carousel and wasn't expecting the two men that greeted me and took my bags. They carried them to the front door of the airport and sat them down. One guy explained that each officer on duty needed $20 and there were five officers working. I think the word is extortion. I felt very intimidated and pulled out two $20 bills handed them to the guy and said, "that is all I have." He smiled and said, "Ok." That's when I knew I'd been suckered.

As I left the airport it felt like walking into another world. An older white couple was in front of the building and they were getting hassled. I talked to them earlier in the airport. They were in Nigeria for mission work.

I was looking for Bisi and she finally emerged from the crowd with a huge smile on her face. She hugged me and immediately went to the rescue of the older couple. They were scared. She calmed them down and called someone on her cell phone to come get them.

That's Bisi. Dressed like an African Queen. Persuasive would not be doing her justice. We found our way through the crowd to a car and driver she had waiting for us.

Riding in a car in Lagos is frightening. That's the only way to put it. Absolutely frightening! An estimated twenty million people live there and it's highway anarchy, with potholes. Anytime there is an obstruction in the road to slow you down someone comes running up to your car to sell something. It's capitalism at work, but it's still crazy.

It took us two hours to drive to the Sickle Cell Association building in the compound where I would be staying. It was directly across the street from the Lagos University Teaching Hospital.

Bisi took great care of me, always making sure the car she hired was air-conditioned and the drivers were very helpful.

My first event was the following morning at the Pan African University. It was a beautiful facility but the heavy rain kept most people home.

Food became a major issue. I struggled with the chicken and rice that was served at every meal my first 48 hours. Plantains, oh my goodness. Never again will I eat another plantain.

Day three in Nigeria, I became ill with some kind of stomach issue. By lunchtime, a knock came at my door. Bisi's sister introduced herself; she was a nurse at the Teaching Hospital across the street. She walked in and behind her was a doctor. He was fantastic! His family lives in Dallas and he commutes. He gave me an antibiotic and by the next morning I was fine. Bisi came to pick me up and we went searching for food I could eat. We found a donut shop and I pigged out. No milk though. Coffee! Yaaaaaa! I also bought a canned Coke, also a rarity.

Day 4, today all we had to do was go to the Silverbird Television Studio and tape an interview. Bisi showed up with a different car and driver. Again we crossed Lagos after a downpour. We turned down the road leading to the studio and had to abandon our car and driver because the potholes, now full of water, would have swallowed our car. There were boards to walk on to stay out of the mud. We walked for five minutes when Bisi and I got lucky. Two young ladies in a Ford Explorer braving the deep trenches gave us a lift.

Day 5, Bisi and I flew to Abuja, the capitol of Nigeria. My next event was at the Hilton Hotel on

Thursday night. The honored guest at the event was Chief Solomon Lar and his wife, Mary.

Chief Lar is a Nigerian politician who held various offices at the national level for over fifty years. He was the founding chairman of the Peoples Democratic Party which has held power since the return to democracy in 1999.

Chief Solomon Lar, Mary Lar & Michael Clancy at the Abuja Hilton

His wife, Mary Lar, was Nigeria's Ambassador to the Netherlands in 2004.

There were about 100 people in attendance and the hostess began to introduce the speaker. "You may have noticed there is someone in the crowd that is very different from the rest of us. Yes, ladies and gentlemen, it's the white guy! Michael Clancy is our speaker for the evening," she said.

It was very refreshing to be around people that have no concept of racism as we in the U.S. know it. My visit to Nigeria taught me the difference between racism and prejudice.

The event went well and Chief Lar asked if I would like to attend church services with he and his wife on Sunday. "Yes, absolutely," I replied. "Do you know his church?" Bisi asked. "No", I said. "His church is Aso Villa Chapel, the private chapel for the President of Nigeria." Wow! How exciting.

Saturday I was scheduled to speak at a church in Keffi, 60 kilometers from Abuja. The church was the Evangelical Church of West Africa and it was a tribal church. A generator was used to supply electricity for the event.

Picture previous page, Michael Clancy at the Evangelical Church of West Africa in Keffi, Nigeria, September 11, 2010

I was told as I walked in I was welcome to photograph whatever I wanted. I took out my video camera and captured part of the worship service. It was a women's conference and very few men were present. The pastor acted as an interpreter and I fear a lot was lost in the translation. A collective gasp came from the audience when my baby's hand picture appeared on the screen.

Tears welled up in my eyes as I again realized how big God is. He brought me across the world to a church in Africa to share my story.

Bisi said, "Be ready to give your presentation at Aso Villa Chapel tomorrow, it might not happen, just be ready."

The next morning we arrived at the President's Chapel and the security was what you'd expect. We went through at least three checkpoints and my AV equipment was taken at the last one. We entered the sanctuary and the service had already begun.

The President of Nigeria, President Goodluck Jonathan, was speaking at the podium as we found our seats. We sat in the second row, behind Chief Lar and his wife.

A time came during the service when visitors were recognized. My name was called and as I stood everyone clapped. I said I was visiting with Lifechoice International. About fifteen others were introduced but Bisi was skipped over. I could see the disappointment on her face. Mary Lar wrote on a piece of paper and handed it to the usher.

Shortly after an announcement was made that someone had been overlooked. Bisi was introduced as the President of Lifechoice International and a guest of Chief Lar. She stood and shouted, "Praise The Lord." Again Bisi was glowing and it was clear this was a highlight in her life.

We didn't get to meet the President but we met his chaplain, the Venerable Obioma Onwuzurumba. I presented him with a copy of my picture and Bisi and I had our photograph taken with him.

My visit to Nigeria was very emotional. Again, I couldn't help but see God at work. Bisi said to me,

"Michael, it is because of you we worshipped at the president's chapel."

The following day was my last in Nigeria. I really wanted to pick up a few more gifts for Juanita. I mentioned this to Bisi and she asked about the dress I'd already bought. "I was hoping to find some handmade jewelry for her to wear with the dress, nothing expensive," I said. "Do you want to go to the cultural village?" Bisi asked. "No, it's too much of a tourist trap, it'll be ok. At least I have something for her," I said.

Bisi Chukwudile, Venerable Obioma Onwuzurumba, Michael Clancy at Aso Villa Chapel

Bisi waited to rally our driver, Vincent, for my trip to the airport. I would miss my flight if we didn't hurry. I had to fly back to Lagos before my 12-hour flight to Atlanta. It was really getting late and it seemed as though she was stalling. A car pulled into the compound and it was Bisi's cohorts. They came in and surprised me with all sorts of handmade jewelry that would pair well with the dress. I was overwhelmed by their generosity and again brought to tears as we said our goodbyes.

I had mixed emotions about going to Nigeria and after getting the stomach flu all I truly wanted to do was go home.

But I would have missed all this. I will never forget the incredible people I met and in the end it was the trip of a lifetime.

17 MAX AGUILERA-HELLWEG

Just as the Life Magazine family is very important to my story so is the photographer who took the picture for their article, Max Aguilera-Hellweg. I Googled him and found his web site. I didn't notice a way to contact him at first, but I was still too timid to try. I didn't feel the time was right.

A year earlier I emailed Skip Hollandsworth, author of the Life Magazine article, at Texas Monthly. He worked there as an editor. He never responded. I couldn't take a chance the same thing would happen if I emailed Max.

Years earlier I asked a friend, Matt Archbold, to call him at a phone number I found on www.zabasearch.com to ask him certain questions.

Later that same night I received an email from Matt. It said, "I couldn't believe it, I called the number you gave me and on the second ring he answered. As I talked to him everything you've told me came out. It was incredible. I wrote my notes in shorthand so it'll take me a bit to go through it all but here are the relevant quotes for now."

The following quote was by Max Aguilera-Hellweg, June 2003:

"The picture was discussed to be on the cover but when his (Clancy's) story broke it took the wind out of our story .... it stole the thunder from a really great picture ..... he (Hellweg) thought he witnessed something miraculous ..... the whole thing was very upsetting to me. I mean to have that picture appear after I had shot mine .... It was upsetting to me because some people said and I mean photo editors said he (Clancy) was the real photojournalist because mine was posed and they put mine down. Life Magazine had fears all along that the photo, well, it could be misinterpreted and it could be used by the pro-life movement but we didn't want to exploit the picture."

Matt went on to say,

"Michael, these are unbelievable quotes."

Wow! That says everything! Life Magazine photo editors knew my picture was real. I couldn't help but wonder what Dr. Bruner told the editors at Life

Magazine. Did he tell them he couldn't stop me from getting the picture?

After Max took the picture of Sarah Marie Switzer he decided he wanted to, "be the guy saving other people's lives." He put himself through medical school and graduated from Tulane University School of Medicine, Class of 2004.

Did Hellweg ever become a practicing physician? I searched and searched.

I found the following in a bio for Hellweg on www.nationalgeographic.com. He was apparently shooting pictures for them.

Bio: Max Aguilera-Hellweg, Photographer

"Just a month shy of his 18th birthday, Max was hired by Rolling Stone magazine to work in its darkroom and assist chief photographer Annie Leibovitz when she was in town. Aguilera-Hellweg began to take his own photos, including a shot of a young bodybuilder named Arnold Schwarzenegger. Aguilera-Hellweg's clients have included Fortune, Time, Esquire, Rolling Stone, GEO, Stern, Discover, Scientific American, Details, Connoisseur, Newsweek, the Washington Post Magazine, the Los Angeles Times Magazine, the New York Times Magazine, Texas Monthly, the New Yorker, and many other magazines. His first story for National Geographic was on stem cell research in July 2005."

I knew the picture of Arnold the bio referred to. It was on the cover of a bodybuilding magazine I'd had for years. That photo now hangs in The Museum of Modern Art in New York.

He was back to shooting pictures. Why did he put himself through medical school and not follow through by becoming a practicing physician? Then I found an article on www.docs.google.com regarding his experience:

"Bully-Busting Basics" by Susan Sarver

"Max greatly anticipated his third-year surgical rotation. However, the rotation became a lesson in intimidation. The intern dogged him on all his duties for the first two days and pushed Aguilera-Hellweg physically. "If I couldn't answer a question correctly he would shove himself into me. Because I had been told by the administration not to say anything, I held back." With the support of a few upper-level medical residents, he found the courage to tell the intern to stop pushing him around. When he reported the new level of abuse to one of deans who had advised against reporting the behavior, Aguliera-Hellweg was removed from the service." Despite the new assignment he was treated as an outcast. He was so traumatized by his surgical rotation his confidence plummeted. In a letter he eventually sent to two administrators, Aguilera-Hellweg described the learning atmosphere: "Daily

*there is an air of intimidation, ridicule, and spite."
In closing, he added, I hope that drafting this letter
will somehow begin to heal me and serve to
address these individuals for no other student or
patient should suffer their brutality and
unprincipled behavior."*

After reading the article I couldn't have been more
convinced that now was the time to contact Max.
Bullying is exactly what happened to me. Dr. Bruner
inviting me into the operating room and having me
assaulted in order to stop me from getting a picture
of the hand when it was thrust out of the surgical
opening was bullying. He would understand why I
was fighting so hard for my picture.

February 2, 2011 I spent two hours writing,
erasing, and re-writing a short email to Max and
sent it at 10:25 in the morning. At 10:27, two
minutes later, he answered. He was extremely nice
in his response and said he would be happy to talk
to me but his schedule wouldn't allow it until some
time in March. I asked him to let me know when he
had free time coming up.

March and April passed and I didn't hear from
Max. I did two events for the Vitae Foundation in
Missouri and had several weeks before another
event. I emailed him again on May 5, 2011. I told
him Juanita and I were driving to New York City

and asked if he might have an hour to meet with us. He said yes!

Juanita took off work at noon on the 12th of May. We packed and were on the road by 6:30 p.m. Eighteen hours and seven states later we were crossing the George Washington Bridge. We could see New York City off in the distance. Juanita took the video camera out and shot footage. An hour later we arrived at the Hampton Inn in Stamford, Connecticut. We could only sleep a few hours before we woke up hungry. The trusty Garmin led us to a diner where we had jumbo butterfly shrimp. It was fantastic. We also ordered a piece of chocolate cake to go, for each of us.

Juanita turned over to go to sleep at 9:20 and I watched '48 Hours' until 11 p.m.

This was not an ordinary Hampton Inn. It had free underground parking fifty feet from the hotel entrance. The landscaping was immaculate and there was a great looking restaurant adjoining the hotel. When we returned from dinner Tiki torches were lit creating a very romantic atmosphere. Our room had one of a very few balconies overlooking the front entrance. Across the street was a stream with seagulls splashing around.

I woke up abruptly at 12:10 a.m. to the sound of people having an argument in the hallway. I jumped up and ran to look through the peephole. There were several people standing just a few feet away from our door. Juanita called the front desk to report the disturbance and was reassured it would be taken care of. I laid down and before I knew it I fell asleep.

About 1:45 a.m., I was awakened by the sound of a police cruiser siren arriving on the scene. I quickly pulled on my sweats and opened the door to the balcony. I counted seventeen police cars with flashing lights and people everywhere. A late night party in the restaurant had gotten out of hand. I heard Juanita say something and I said, "You've got to see this, bring the video camera." She came out on the balcony with me and I shot footage of the police officers as they tried to calm the crowd. It was 4:30 in the morning when I finally got to sleep again. I couldn't get the impending meeting with Max off my mind.

Juanita and I arrived an hour early at the Starbucks where Max said to meet him. The music inside was incredibly loud and I told Juanita I wanted to sit at the table just outside the door. I brought my digital voice recorder for the interview and the music inside would have drowned out our conversation.

He arrived at exactly 3 p.m. The first thing I said to him was, "I wondered if I would recognize you." Then I said, "I'm so sorry if anything I did caused you any grief. I did what I had to to fight for my picture." A puzzled look came over his face. I told him he was like this mythological character that stood twenty feet tall in my story. He was such a good photographer Life Magazine would hire him for an assignment. He must be the best of the best.

In the first five minutes of our conversation Max used the word "loneliness," three times. I could see the pain in his eyes. He was very gracious in his mannerism, looking at both Juanita and I as he spoke.

He would not discuss people at Life Magazine that worked on the story. I already knew Vivette Porjes was the Photo Editor and he confirmed it when I said her name.

I was amazed to hear his incredible picture was taken with a 4 x 5 camera. No wonder it is so fantastic.

I told him about being grabbed in an attempt to stop me from getting any picture of the hand. He acted surprised to hear that. Although, I suspect he knew as much about me as I knew about him. I've stated in print many places that I was grabbed during the surgery. It's on my web site.

"It was perfect for our story," Max said about his picture. "But if there is another picture like it already published Life Magazine is not going to put it on the cover."

"Do you know what Dr. Bruner told people at Life Magazine that would explain how I was able to capture my picture?" I asked. "No," he said.

During our entire meeting I could feel the elephant in the room. The fact that he and I feel differently about abortion. He actually said, "I know you're Christian," and mentioned George Tiller being gunned down. I knew exactly where he stood. Pro-lifers are crazy people.

At the end of our meeting I reiterated my sorrow for any grief I'd caused him. "I lost the cover. It wasn't anything you did intentionally," Max said. I needed to hear that from him and shake his hand more than anything else.

As we drove away I could not get over his use of the word, "loneliness." Even though newly married, with a new baby, he is still searching.

I couldn't have felt more accomplished after finally meeting Max, twelve years after taking the picture. He was now a real person for me. That part of my journey was over.

Michael Clancy & Max Aguilera-Hellweg outside Starbucks in Stamford, CT

The 16-hour drive home was brutal.

18 BLESSED, CONCLUSION

I promised that in my book I would identify the person that attacked me in the operating room. When I received the emails from Dr. Ray Paschall the first one was copied to Paul Wilson, and Dr. Joseph Bruner. Vanderbilt has Paul Wilson listed as a CRNA-OB/GYN. I believe Paul Wilson was the Certified Registered Nurse Anesthetist for Samuel's surgery and he was the person that grabbed me. The fourth frame of the pictures I was able to capture of Samuel reaching from the womb clearly show Dr. Bruner frantically waving his right hand. I'm convinced Bruner was signaling Paul Wilson to stop me and subsequently, I was attacked. He is pictured on page 56, top right, looking at the camera.

What happened to me as a child is called rape. It should never have happened but it did. I allowed myself to be consumed by hate until the Grace of God covered me and set me free.

It was a big break for me to get the serpent handling assignment, frightening and fascinating all at the same time. I haven't been back since having my tonsils removed and my desire to photograph a service is no more. I did call Peggy in 2005 and she said they now have full custody of their grandchildren. John and Peggy will always have a special place in my heart.

This book is a celebration. Even with the threat of legal action from Dr. Paschall Vanderbilt has not, as of yet, brought any legal action against me.

Life Magazine became so furious with Vanderbilt for telling me their baby was twenty-four weeks in utero; when the article published they weren't on speaking terms.

Dr. Joseph Bruner lied to cover up the truth, Samuel simply came out from under the anesthesia too soon.

I'm sorry to the Switzers, Vanderbilt, Dr. Joseph Bruner, John Howser, Life Magazine, and Max Hellweg. I meant no harm. I was left no other choice but to fight for my picture.

Being the photographer that took the picture of Samuel reaching from his mother's womb has been a journey to the edge of sanity.

To have it in our heart to take the life of an unborn baby as a fix for an unplanned pregnancy will result in the end of civilization, as we know it.

Too often we put people on a pedestal. We expect too much. If you have a father that disappointed you, forgive them. You already have the greatest father anyone could ever want. His name is Jesus Christ and all you have to do is ask and He will set you free.

19 IMPACT

I wanted to document the impact of the picture and Matt Archbold helped me obtain quotes from people involved on both sides of the abortion debate regarding their thoughts of the Baby Samuel photo.

These comments were obtained in 2003:

1) Marie Jo Laroche -Executive Director League for Life Winnipeg, Canada:

"I saw it in the newspaper, 'The Interim." I thought fabulous. What a photo. How can anyone argue that it's not a human being. I like to think of it as the baby is thanking the surgeon, saying 'hey help me out here. Do the right thing. We've used it as a poster. We made up 1,500 of them. I think they're 24 by 18. We've sent them to churches and schools. The response has been fabulous."

2) Patty Nixon -Executive Director Alberta Pro-Life Alliance Association:

"I saw it on the Internet. All I could think was that it's exceptional. The technology is advancing today so quickly. The argument about the baby being a blob of tissue was done the moment that hand reached out. We don't ever have to debate that again. We've used the photo in an exhibit at different events. The first one was at a youth conference in Edmonton with 16,000 people. We've had a very good response. They say pictures are worth a thousand words. In this instance that's true for sure."

3) Lowell Highby -Director of Media and Development Lutherans for Life –Nevada:

"When I saw the photo all I could think was that it's amazing how much denial people are in about this issue. This proves that babies in the womb are not a blob. They never were."

4) Martha Short - Pennsylvanians for Human Life:

"How beautiful, I thought. This is a picture that will save lives. It shows the humanity of the unborn baby. And it gives us more ammunition in our efforts to stop abortion." We show it in all our classes. We've had it for 2 + years. It's laminated and we pass it around in classes. The reaction is overwhelming. Just last year we showed it to 32,000 people in 120 schools, parochial and public and the students have been receptive. We've received so many letters just about this photograph.

5) Phyliss Kinsler, President and CEO of Planned Parenthood in Central New Jersey:

Is it amazing, wonderful and spectacular? You bet it is. But does it outweigh all the other issues such as the trauma related to a crisis pregnancy? I don't think so. It must be a balancing act. It definitely helps anti abortion activists in their work -especially with young people...

Almost everyone knows someone going through a high-risk pregnancy that is now someone's beloved niece or nephew. The other side is that many of us know women who have almost lost their lives trying to deliver a really non-viable fetus. We can't impose our determination. When you look at pictures of truly fragile preemies they don't look like the perfectly formed in-utero pictures they show. It's not quite as romantic. They tend to romanticize the fetus. We have to worry about the pain and suffering for that infant as well as the parents worrying about it. Let's remember that agony. What's not showing in that photo and many of the others is the woman that the fetus is in. No ones' talking about what's a blob of tissue is or isn't. The question is whether fetal personhood and fetal rights should override the women involved. I think most people would agree to allow women to be part of that determination."

6) Kathleen Sweeney Publication and Research Coordinator for National Right to Life Coalition:

"The first time I saw it was when somebody put it up on the wall in my office. I was amazed. I think everybody was amazed."

7) Trent Frank - Republican Congressman (AZ):

"A pro-life friend of mine sent it to me on an email in 2002. I think it came out a few years before that but when I saw it, it sure had a profound impact on me and I think everyone who has seen it. I absolutely applaud the people who brought this picture to the world. I pray that somehow it will be part of the awakening of our nation and that someday that we will look back with the profoundest darkest sorrow. The pro-abortion lobby continues to lose credibility because more and more people are becoming aware of the humanity of the baby. This photo removes all reasonable doubt that this is a child. The real question is does abortion kill a baby? Then this is a non issue. Once people realize that abortion really does kill a baby this will be considered the greatest human holocaust in the history of humanity. The picture of little Samuel Armas was so poignant and so powerful It's like this little hand is reaching out to all of us. I believe the hand of hope is reaching out to those of us who have the power to respond. If we don't in a sense it dehumanizes all of us. It's not the dying that leaves scars. It's the killing. And there are 43 million scars in this country. The very core purpose of the law, the very reason the law exists is the intrinsic understanding that innocent human beings should have their rights protected from those that are stronger and would arbitrarily desecrate them. That's so basic to this country. But people in this case are saying it's outside the law. We're never quite so eloquent as when we're talking about past tragedies. We wonder now how people could have lost sight of compassion so badly that we perpetrated the immoral act of slavery in this country. Now we've killed 43 million children."

8) Kate Michelman- President of the National Abortion and Reproductive Rights Action League (NY Times 2001):

"It does make our job harder because the images are very powerful, and they get used and abused in this hostile way."

9) Lorraine Pierotti, Director of Advocacy Planned Parenthood Northeast Pennsylvania:

"The pictures that have been shown in Newsweek and the pictures some people promote are always of what looks like babies - well formed and well developed. Look, there's a big difference between a fertilized egg and a six-month fetus. These pictures are for lack of a better word sexier than talking about the woman. As things become more and more complex - roe v wade makes more and more sense. Childbearing choices are constitutionally protected. More protected earlier than later. In the 3rd trimester a state may take the fetus into consideration. Roe v wade still does make sense. People look at a picture without any context. Most people don't read a whole newspaper or magazine article. How many people do you think just glanced at the photo. And they're not getting the whole story. They just look and say 'yup that's a baby.' But no matter who that person is when it comes to that time in their life they will consider abortion. It doesn't mean they'll choose it. But they will consider it. It's just a basic human response."

10) Maria Vitale - Education Director Pro-Life Federation:

"Because of that picture I was able to see the strength and humanity of the unborn child in a way I hadn't seen it before. The idea that this child reached out and held on for dear life is just awesome. This photo is making a terrific impact because once you see it, it's difficult to deny the humanity of an unborn child deserving as much love and protection as anybody else. I think people were lied to about abortion for so long. They were told it's just a blob of tissue. This photograph shows that to be a lie. I believe if you present this photo to everyone, the vast majority of people would be pro-life. I think so many people would say, 'My Gosh, I didn't realize." This picture I believe is very responsible for the shift in the polls. It has given us a window to the womb.

11) Marilyn Musgrave (R) Colorado:

"When I was in the state Senate in Colorado, my daughter who was a Legislative Assistant brought the picture to me. I showed to all my fellow legislators. It touches everyone's heart that sees it. What they do with that feeling is up to them. Do they harden their hearts to it or open themselves to it? But for those with a tender heart it will affect them greatly. There's a very vulnerable human being in that picture. There's something so beguiling so touching about it. We know in our culture we reach out our hand for help or in thankfulness or just to reach out to be close. That baby reached out. It reminds me of a story. My father in law had open-heart surgery. He was going through a crisis. We all went to visit him. We took my grandchild. She reached out to him. He said, "I can't lift that little baby up. Someone put that baby on my lap." It's a very human emotion. It's undeniably a precious vulnerable human being making contact with the doctor. The picture has given us a window to the womb. When you look at this photo you can't take your eyes off it. I believe that there's been a shift in the way the country looks at abortion because of this picture and some others. The picture has made a difference because it forces us to confront reality."

12) Susan Meyers-Campus Minister:

"I saw a copy of the picture in the Saint Louis Review and the only word I can come up to describe my feeling is awe. I use it in my slide presentation for 5th and 6th graders. I just think you can't honestly be pro-choice after seeing this picture. I don't know how people who are pro-choice square it with their conscience. I have no doubt that the shift in the polls towards the pro-life side is due to this picture. Before this picture the only thing pro-lifers had to show were gruesome pictures of aborted children. Pictures like that inspire anger and could make people do harm to us. But a picture like baby Samuel the only emotion, a realization that this is a life and not a mass of matter."

13) Lori Hougens-National Right to Life spokesperson:

"The picture is spectacular. It has opened the eyes of countless people who would never have contemplated the full humanity of the unborn. The pro-abortion movement's success depends on keeping people in the dark. Because of this photo we've seen polls change and hearts change. When people learn the truth – their hearts change."

ABOUT THE AUTHOR

Michael Clancy was a photojournalist in the Middle Tennessee
area for 20 years. Witnessing Samuel reach from the womb
changed everything for him and began an incredible journey.
Few are blessed to witness such a moment and even fewer are
willing to sacrifice everything for the world to know the truth.

www.michaelclancy.com

Made in the USA
Charleston, SC
11 March 2012